Ordinarily, opening pages
recommendations for the auth[o]
people recovering from drug a[?]
Author - of life and salvation.

In praise of Jesus:

"I used to be hopeless and lost, a monster I didn't know or like. Now I'm joyful and peaceful, a wonderful mother, wife, daughter, and friend. I give all glory to you, Jesus, for being the light in my world of darkness, for completely restoring my life. Forever grateful and blessed," – Tarah

"I love you, Jesus, for loving me when I couldn't love myself. Thank you for putting light back into my eyes when everything was dark. I'm truly blessed." – Schyler

"I love Jesus because He has changed me for the better and made me who I am. He gave me life and let the real me come out. He gave me the strength to put a smile on other people's faces and to give me the joy to see that! Thank You. I love You, God." – Ashlynne

"God had His own Son, Jesus Christ, to die on the cross for us, for our sins. That just shows how much God really loves us. Thank You!" – Laurin

"When I was broken and bleeding, the Lord knit me together and set me on my feet again." – Brad

"I turned away from God in my addiction and yet He still rescued me from my addiction. I was dead in my addiction, but now, by the grace of God, I am alive." – Devon

"It has taken six felonies, five trips to the Department of Corrections, the loss of my grandparents and my mother to cause me to start looking for God. And then, it only took me finding fifty cents while I was living in a homeless shelter to show me He loves me." – Marcus

"When I try to explain how God changed my life to others, they sometimes cannot relate. But when I talk about Jesus to those of us who God has taken out of the dark into the light, it is the best feeling in the world – just to talk about Him with them. It is because we KNOW how He has changed our lives. I cannot speak for anybody else, but for me, God is awesome." – Amos

"I spent twenty-six years of my life as a drug addict and I never really believed in God until now. I am sober and alive today and I thank God." – Mindi

Steps one foods

Jesus and
the Addict

Dr. Pam Morrison

CONTENTS

Acknowledgements

ACKNOWLEDGMENTS

I wish to thank two beautiful ladies, Bobbi Jo Reed, and Judi Burkholder, the "moms" of the Healing House Recovery Community in Kansas City, Missouri. Their wonderful faith and tremendous love for people in recovery is inspiring and a model for bold ministry.

I thank my dear friend, Pastor Tom Langhofer, who has given me many opportunities to teach at the Healing House during the Friday night gatherings.

I wish to say thank you to the countless men and women that I have met and with whom I have had the privilege of ministering in recovery facilities, jails, churches, and at the Healing House. It is hard to say who was helped more by these relationships, them or me! I am grateful to witness their courage and to receive their love.

And, as always, I am so thankful to my dear husband, David, who has supported me in every adventure with God. Thank you, David

Introduction

Several years ago, I was appointed pastor of a church that hosted various community groups, among them, an Alcoholics Anonymous Group (AA) that met in the basement. The AA group kept their rented room neat and tidy; chairs ringed the room, a coffee pot rested on a rolling cart, and posters encouraging sobriety adorned the walls. The only fault of the group, if one was looking for faults, was the constant, pungent smell of cigarette smoke in the room, even though the members smoked outside, and the fact that, well, they were there.

Periodically, the Administrative Board of the church would meet in the dark-paneled church library and someone would bring up the AA group asking, "Isn't it time we had them leave and meet somewhere else? After all, they only give us twenty-five dollars a month for rent!!" Granted, that was twenty-five dollars a month more than any of the Sunday school classes, Bible studies, or various other community groups – but there was something about having AA in their church building that seemed, for some, to be "stuck in their craw." Saying, "we need the space," was not *really* what lay beneath the eviction talk. This was a staid, traditional, non-growing church. Somewhere in their collective heart, it appeared they found it indelicate to have smoking ex-drunks and drug users coming into their holy building.

It was striking, but not surprising, that only two or three of the recovering addicts were seen participating in the life of the church, coming to worship, or joining a small group. The tension over them was one of many battles that can occur in a church community, and I did not deal with this one head on, I regret to say. I didn't fully understand it at the time, nor was I the advocate of those escaping addiction that I would later become. I did not understand the needs of the church members as well as I should have either. I needed to grow.

Now, years later, having spent much time with many addicts in recovery, I wonder, "How could a church congratulate itself on being broad-minded by hosting an Alcoholics Anonymous group, but never feel it important or part of the gospel to joyfully woo them upstairs and bring them into the full life of the church community? How could they not go beyond the walls of the church and bring even *more* in since God was highlighting this opportunity?"

Could it be that that church's ideas about God, the cross, and people were way off the mark from where Jesus, in His love, would have had them be? Were they lacking the love of Christ's heart? And I am not speaking from the silly and superficial perspective offered by too many from the American church today, "Judge not lest you be judged also - Jesus loves everybody the way they are!" That is silliness to the nth degree! Yes, Jesus loved and accepted people. Yes, He mingled constantly with sinners. But He *also* radically delivered them out of their fallen lifestyles. Ultimately, He died on the cross to deliver us all from sin and death into salvation and life. He wants to move humanity from death to life. That was His mission! "The reason the Son of God appeared was to destroy the devil's work." (1 John 3:8 NIV) Therefore, Jesus radically loved those addicts in recovery in the basement just as He radically loved the uptight, sometimes unsaved people (yes, unsaved) upstairs. He desires for us all to encounter Him and be radically transformed by *His salvation*, not by our self-effort, to resemble Him. He wants us to let Him love us His way, His sovereign way - the chosen in Christ "before the foundation of the world" way (Eph. 1:4-5 NIV) – so that out of this, with a new life and restored identity, *given by grace*, we might love others.

Truly, only those who call upon the name of the Lord in total dependence, believing in His finished work on the cross for them, are saved, and it is the same for everyone. We're set free because of Him, not because of us, our thinking, our good works, or our managing to "keep quiet and unseen" anything someone else might construe as bad. We stand on level ground before the cross of Christ, or we should! No church should be haughty and unwelcoming to those struggling with drugs and resultant poverty by hoisting an unseen, but strongly felt sign saying, "Your kind not welcome here." (Yet, it is compassionately understood that training in how to minister to this population is immeasurably valuable. More valuable and above all else, is the anointing and guidance of the Holy Spirit who gives us wisdom.)

We are all the same kind - people depraved and condemned without Jesus – dead! And I'm not sure which "dead" person Jesus pities more – the addict lost in addiction or the respectable person lost in self-righteousness and isolation from those they consider beneath them. The delusion that our good works, aside from Jesus, make us right with God leads us to frustrated striving and judgment of others. That self-righteousness is ignorant and rigid, revealing a lack of knowing God and even a disdain for Him. It needs healing, kindness, and redemption, too.

Freeing people from the captivity of addiction should be among the missions of the Church as it ministers to a lost and needy world. The National Institute on Drug Addiction (NIDA), part of the National Institutes of Health (NIH) in the US, periodically publishes statistics on drug addiction. Consider these three statements from their website about drug use in the US[1]:

Abuse of tobacco, alcohol, and illicit drugs is costly to our Nation, exacting more than $740 billion annually in costs related to crime, lost work productivity, and health care.

In 2013 an estimated 24.6 million Americans ages 12 or older – 9.4 percent of the population – had used an illicit drug in the past month.

There continues to be a large treatment gap in this country. In 2013, an estimated 22.7 million Americans (8.6 percent) needed treatment for a problem related to drugs or alcohol, but only about 2.5 million people (0.9 percent) received treatment at a specialty facility.

I would argue that the single greatest resource for redirecting a life and healing its brokenness, including addiction, is being far under-utilized. That resource is the Son of God. "So if the Son sets you free, you will be free indeed," (John 8:36 NIV) is the glorious promise of the gospel of John. Our approaches to addiction recovery have often been more secular and medical. All this is useful, but Jesus Christ has a track record of radically and totally freeing people by transforming their lives. More importantly, He is the path to life eternal. My hope is to see Christian recovery efforts spread enormously throughout this country and wherever needed, in the rest of the world.

We, addicts and non-addicts alike, ought to be in the sanctuary praising God together, talking in small groups together, doing works of community service together. That is my hope and my prayer that Christ-followers begin to recover or understand for the first time that "there is now a righteousness apart from the Law" as is stated in Romans 3:21. It is a righteousness that we receive through Christ alone. But let's "hear" it described in the beautiful, and easy to grasp language of The Living Bible Translation:

> But now God has shown us a different way to heaven – not by "being good enough" and trying to keep his laws, but by a new way (though not new, really, for the Scriptures told about it long ago). Now God says he will accept and acquit us - declare us "not guilty" – if we trust Jesus Christ to take away our sins. And we all can be saved in this same way, by coming to Christ, no matter who we are or what we have been like. Yes, all have sinned; all fall short of God's glorious ideal; yet now God declares us "not guilty" of offending him if we trust in Jesus Christ, who in his kindness freely takes away our sins. (Romans 3:21-24 TLB)

Jesus Christ is the answer to every human failing, including and especially, addiction.

This text contains Bible lessons utilized in a Christian recovery setting. They have been used as interim studies between sessions of the Alpha Christian evangelistic program. Alpha is designed to teach the basics of the Christian faith in a non-threatening, pleasant environment where any question about faith is welcome and legitimate. Topics include things like: "Who is Jesus?" "Why Did He Die?" "How Do I Pray?" and so on.

The hope is that through Alpha (or another evangelistic program), addicted people will be enabled to find and receive Christ, be filled with the Holy Spirit, and experience the healing power of Jesus coming between them and the enslavement of addiction. However, even though our spirit is made perfect forever in the moment or process of salvation, we still need to be sanctified (Hebrews 10:14) and have our soul (mind, will, and emotions) healed and matured. (Romans 12:2) That is the intention of the author through this leader's guide – to provide "soul-healing" Bible studies that are particularly relevant to the needs of recovering addicts. In these pages, issues such as conquering fear, having perseverance, healing old wounds, renewing hope, and dealing with many other challenges are addressed. And as always, the nature of God as loving Father, Son, and Holy Spirit is reiterated among these other subjects.

Each study session has a key verse or verses, a background discussion of the topic (so that a speaker may reflect on the group's needs while preparing a talk), a sample talk, and discussion questions for the breakout small groups which may meet after a leader's presentation. The sample talk is meant to give you a template. Change the stories, personalize it, make it your own, even highlight other points. The sample is just to stir your creativity and imagination. Let the Holy Spirit help you to make the talk your own.

Being yourself is so important, even if your background is vastly different from the people you serve. I think often of David

Wilkerson, the pastor who authored *The Cross and the Switchblade*. He went from a quiet family church in Pennsylvania to the teenage street gangs of New York to minister. He was totally different in background from those he served and grew to love so deeply. What equipped him? Did he have to become an addict or a lawbreaker to relate to them? That is often the prevailing wisdom – that only an addict can help an addict.

No, he did not change. He went to this call from God very naïve and some might say, unqualified, simply saying, "Yes, God." It was the Holy Spirit in him who qualified him and gave him the wisdom and power he needed to relate to the people he served.

I have heard people come and speak to recovery communities and attempt to act in the way they feel will be expected trying to sound cool and using a little street language to fit in. If that is not you, don't do it! Be yourself. Authenticity is always better. The audience we are really trying to please is our Father in heaven by being a sincere servant of His plans for saving people. Just love them. Present the truth. God will do the rest.

I have used a variety of Biblical translations for the scriptures quoted. As many do, I capitalize the first letter of pronouns out of reverence for God, but do not do this within quotes if it is not the practice of the writers of a particular translation.

And now, may God bless every good intention of your heart, as you continue in recovery ministry or undertake it for the first time to make the community of Christ what it was intended to be – a place where Mary Magdalene, Matthew, Peter, Nicodemus, Joseph of Arimathea, rabbis, lepers, thieves, and prostitutes all find their way home together.

1
The Love of the Father

Key Verses

> And you did not receive the "spirit of religious duty," leading you back into the fear *of never being good enough.* But you have received the "Spirit of full acceptance," enfolding you into the family of God. And you will never feel orphaned, for as he rises up within us, our spirits join him in saying the words of tender affection, "Beloved Father, Abba!" For the Holy Spirit makes God's fatherhood real to us as he whispers into our innermost being: "You are God's beloved child!" (Romans 8:15-16 TPT)

> "You are accepted in the Beloved." (Ephesians 1:6 NKJV)

Issues for the Speaker to consider

What is the family background of the addict? Well, clearly, there can be a wide variety of backgrounds dependent on so many things: class, ethnicity, marital status of parents, education, father's and mother's sobriety or lack of it, etc. One size does not fit all. It goes without saying, you need to understand who your audience is. That may come the natural way – you are speaking to people you know – or the Holy Spirit way – God reveals the needs in front of you. In either case, prayer and listening for God's voice help. Take time to truly be alone with the Father and hear His heart for you. Hear His heart for the people in front of you. Out of the overflow of His love will come the love you need to help the people in your unique recovery setting.

I have interacted mostly with addicts from families of lower socio-economic backgrounds. We know, however, from the nightly news that addiction is no respecter of persons. How many times have we seen the tearful interview of parents or other family members who have lost a loved one to overdose? Fentanyl, heroin, opioids, methamphetamines, these words are too commonly found sprinkled in our national conversations. From the poorest urban and rural communities to the suburbs and city streets of the middle class and the wealthy- no area has escaped. We need healing from this blight.

There are those who began drug use at an early age, many times with the use of either marijuana or alcohol which then led to other drugs. Too often the one introducing them to the drug life has been a close family member, even a parent. Sexual abuse, rape, and/or other forms of violence from family and non-family members are also a part of the stories I hear. Many people turn to addiction because of severe childhood trauma and pain. Their traumatic memories are heart-wrenching and disturbing.

Addiction has been a way to self-medicate the painful memories and feelings from these difficult backgrounds. At the same time, it must be remembered that not every person chooses drugs just to deal with pain. There can be a measure of rebellion or thrill seeking that is at work for some. To be truly helpful, you must consider all sorts of possible variables being present in an individual's life and in their drug addiction. And though drug use was a choice in the beginning, it becomes an illness and slavery that seems almost impossible to escape. Those addicted can feel extremely hopeless about getting free from it.

Some addicts have had ties to churches through their families – a variety of church types, with different relatives, helping them to make the connection. And, I have met those who are already Christians yet are still struggling with addiction. But, mostly, I have found many people brand new to the recovery community do not have a background in the church. Often, their understanding of Christianity is rather deistic and/or legalistic. They believe there is a God of some sort but that He is distant and stern. When I ask many of these addicts about their understanding of God, they often will say something very vague and swiftly change the subject. Alcoholics Anonymous and other similar groups may contribute to this vagueness, asking that their participants only search for and find a personal Higher Power. "God can be anything you want," is, many times, what they are told. "Your definition of God will be good enough."

The motivation for framing belief this way in AA, after its having been birthed by Christian connected founders, was that the AA organization wanted to help any desperately addicted person from any type of religious background or those having no religion. This wanting to help anyone and everyone is noble and has been a source of welcome to thousands upon thousands of people around the world. Many would not have crossed the threshold into an AA meeting if they thought there were certain religious requirements. And, perhaps they have had an unhappy history with Christians or other faith traditions. (I will say more about that later.) But, here's the problem. We are not helped by a vague God created from our own imaginations. To receive divine help, a person needs to truly encounter the living God as He is and be helped in the way He wants to help us. God, Himself, offers some thoughts about this that are rather humorous.

In Isaiah 44:16-17 (NIV), God speaks through the prophet Isaiah about an odd thing He has noticed. God comments about how idols are created, that is, gods of our own imaginations and making. As He reflects about the wood a man uses while making his idol, He says:

Half of the wood he burns in the fire; over it he prepares his meal, he roasts his meat and eats his fill. He also warms himself and says, "Ah! I am warm; I see the fire." From the rest he makes a god, his idol; he bows down to it and worships. He prays to it and says, "Save me! You are my god!"

The point is clearly made. If you take a log and burn one end to roast your dinner and then you put gold paint on the other end to worship, how can you think you have encountered anything more than a log?

Making up an idea of God that suits us may feel comfortable at first, but it leaves us ultimately defenseless and unaided. In the passage above, God is not saying, "I condemn you for this." He is saying a god of your own invention cannot and will not help you. It will be a log. The rest of the Bible tells us of His heart, and He says, "The god you make up cannot help you, but I will. Come home." There is potential danger in teaching that whatever we want to think about God is just fine if people do not move off that starting point. But certainly, to open a door, it is gracious and so important to say, "Come as you are, with what you understand now. You are welcome here."

The question, "Do you know who Jesus is?" may be met with confusion and many questions.

> **Making up an idea of God that suits us may feel comfortable at first, but it leaves us ultimately defenseless and unaided.**

"How can one God have different Persons within Him?" "Isn't Jesus just a created, lesser being?" "Aren't all religions the same?" "Is Jesus even real?" I have had all these questions asked of me. And, again, besides that, there is the underlying thought that God is a moody Being. Many have the idea that God is responsible for their suffering and even all the sad consequences of addiction, the loss of their children, their incarceration, and so on. Many think, on some level, that He is a Punisher and a Teacher who uses great adversity to shape our minds. At the very least, they may think He is just indifferent.

All this is to say, the struggle to portray God the Father as loving and as One whose intentions are good towards His creation is challenging. Even calling God "father" (though we understand part of the intention of Jesus in doing that was to draw us into the intimacy He shared) has its drawbacks. Some in recovery may bristle at the word "father" because they have been too hurt and/or abandoned by a human father or their understanding of God is so negative.

What do I mean by "their understanding of God the Father is too negative." Many people, addicted or not, see "the Father" as the punitive One. Jesus dies on the cross and covers us with His righteousness, but the Father looking on is "still an angry deity," and the only thing that keeps Him from annihilating us with thunderbolts is the resurrected Jesus now standing in the way. Wrong! The atonement is taught that way too often, but wrong!! When one reads scripture rightly, we see that the Father loves us

JESUS AND THE ADDICT

dearly as does the Son. He valued us so much – that is why He saved us through the cross. Jesus prayed this beautiful prayer:

> I am not praying for these alone, but also for the future believers who will come to me because of the testimony of these…so that the world will know you sent me and will understand that you love them as much as you love me. (John 17:20, 23 TLB)

More will be said of this verse in the sample talk included in this chapter.

God the Father loves us with the central and most profound demonstration of His love being the incarnation of Jesus, His death on the cross, and His resurrection back to life. God loves us beyond all understanding. He treasures us. He wants us back. He wants to save us in body, mind, and spirit. He desires intimate relationship with us. And we need to urgently communicate this truth everywhere. Eternal matters are at stake.

"For this is how much God loved the world—he gave his one and only, unique Son *as a gift*. So now everyone who believes in him will never perish but experience everlasting life." (John 3:16 TPT)

Proving the love of the Father for us, and for the recovering audience with whom you share this talk, is challenging, but *so* important. Breakthrough in this

> **God the Father loves us with the central and most profound demonstration of His love being the incarnation of Jesus.**

area requires much behind the scenes prayer, compassion, good stories, and strong biblical grounding for your talk.

Prayer for the Speaker and the Talk

Precious Father,

I pray for the one preparing for this time of discussing Your character and Your love. May they be filled with a deep sense of Your caring specifically for them. May the remembrance of Your covenant cut with Christ on Calvary on our behalf, fill their hearts. May every word of scripture that declares "the steadfast love of the Lord endures forever," may every word of every worship song that has praised Your fatherly heart stir in this speaker now as he or she prepares to bring the good news that Jesus came to reveal the *heart* of the Father. As Jesus was and is, so are You. And we can boldly approach Your throne of grace as believers expecting two things and nothing less – mercy and grace. In Jesus' name, Amen

Sample Talk: (Remember, use your own stories and examples as desired.)

Introduction

The Bible tells us that God is one, but He presents Himself to us as three Persons. They are known as the Father, the Son, and the Holy Spirit. Tonight, I simply want to talk about the Father. But talking about Him and using the word "Father," can raise some problems for some of us. Let me tell you about my own experience.

Like many people, I had a struggle in my relationship with my dad, with both parents actually. I felt ignored as the usually well-behaved middle child and criticized as a skinny, shy girl who never seemed to act or look just right in their eyes. As a child, I was not very impressive. They seemed disappointed.

My father could be a bit like a volcano. Most of the time, he was peaceful, but occasionally, he would explode. Storming down the hall because a radio was too loud or behaving in some other menacing way, we were fearful of him. I remember a time he became so angry with me that he reached over to hit my hand with his fork and broke my dinner plate in two!

All this being said, he was mostly a good, hard-working man, just distant and often truly physically gone because he was in the military. There was a great deal of pressure on him from his work, and in him, because of his desire to please his own dad.

The unfulfilled longings I had for my parents' love were very strong. I remember clinging to my mother when I left for college, weeping, and losing thirty pounds in those days of preparing to separate.

You have your own memories and undoubtedly some or many that are of far worse loneliness and rejection than mine. Sometimes, those experiences with our parents or other significant adults get all tied up with how we think about God. We think He has similar characteristics of coldness. We think He abandons, punishes, or doesn't protect us.

And yet, God's heart and character are vastly different from our human parents who may have been terrible or perhaps like mine, simply trying to do the best they knew how to do. As a young mother, I remember arguing with my parents one night and telling them how their rejection had hurt me. They were visiting us in our home and the next day my father came downstairs and just put his arms around me. He didn't fight with me or defend himself. How precious that moment of fatherly blessing was. Without words, he was saying, "I DO love you and I am sorry." As he grew older, he became more tender.

We need the blessing of a father so desperately in our lives.

I have to tell you I wish I had said more during my father's lifetime to tell him, "I love you and treasure you. Forgive me also." I want to tell you wherever possible be reconciled to people in your lives, particularly family members, particularly parents. If at all possible, find a way to give and receive forgiveness. You will feel so much freedom afterwards.

But now, let's get on with our talk about God as our Father. Here's the life we can have with him according to the Bible:

...you will never feel orphaned, for as he rises up within us, our spirits join him in saying the words of tender affection, "Beloved Father!" For the Holy Spirit makes God's fatherhood real to us as he whispers into our

JESUS AND THE ADDICT

innermost being: "You are God's beloved child!" (Romans 8:15-16 TPT)

Never Feel Orphaned

This beautiful version of Romans 8:15-16 tells us some wonderful things about what our relationship with God the Father is meant to be. First, it says, "we will never feel orphaned" with Him.

Some of you here today are orphans. Maybe not literally, but you may have a mother and father you haven't been around for a long time. God won't do that to you. You will never feel orphaned with Him. He will never be absent from your life. That is the promise from the Bible.

Maybe you have been homeless. You may have been in and out of foster homes. Your parents may have lost or given up your custody. You may have been very mistreated by one or both parents or by step-parents or by parents' boyfriends or girlfriends.

No matter what your story is, it is different with God. He will never make you an orphan where He is concerned or make you feel like an orphan. You won't be like a foster child with the Father. No, His way is to make you feel a total sense of being wanted and of fully and legitimately belonging to Him.

When you are born again, that means when you come to believe in Jesus Christ, you are spiritually born into God's family, and you enter it as a true son or daughter. You're established as a family member. It is eternal, forever. Always.

God says in His Word, "I have loved you with an everlasting love; I have drawn you with unfailing kindness." (Jeremiah 31:3 NIV) He says, "Can a mother forget the baby at her breast and have no compassion on the child she has borne? Though she may forget, I will not forget you!" (Isaiah 49:15 NIV) And it is written in the Psalms, "Even if my father and mother abandon me, the LORD will hold me close." (Psalm 27:10 NLT) God as your Father will never abandon you. Even if you cannot feel Him, He is there.

He is a Father that loves us totally. God is love. (1 John 4:16 NIV) Love is who He is and it is the atmosphere He brings into our lives. Love is the very air of heaven.

Holy Spirit Rises in Us

You may be saying to yourself, "I was hurt so badly, I'll never get over it. I don't trust anybody, and I sure don't trust God.

Love! Phfffff!"

I want you to understand that the promise of the gospel is that when we say yes to Jesus leading our lives; when we sincerely repent and receive His forgiveness, the next thing He wants us to have is God as the Holy Spirit living in us. Yes, the Holy Spirit will be in you is His promise to us. Jesus said, "for he lives with you and will be in you." (John 14:17 NIV) Jesus went even further and said, "Anyone who loves me will obey my teaching. My Father will love them, and we will come to them and make our home with them." (John 14:23 NIV) There it is! Father, Son, and Holy Spirit will be with us when we trust and believe!

The good news in this is that God changes us from the inside out. The sad, bitter, disappointed, or suspicious person you might have been is going to be replaced by a trusting, loving, gentle, God-connected person. The scripture says, "As the Spirit rises up in us…" In other words, as the Holy Spirit influences you in your heart and mind and softens you while healing those old wounds, you're going to find yourself being able to say, "Beloved Father, Abba!" to God. "Abba" was a word Jesus used and it means Papa.

When you can say to God, "Father, Beloved, Papa," you will know your heart has been deeply worked upon by the Spirit, separating your ideas about human parents from God who is nothing like human parents. He is pure love, pure goodness, pure faithfulness, pure justice. He is everything wonderful. He is a wonderful Papa. The Holy Spirit will supernaturally help you to get to the point where you can sincerely feel these things towards God and say them.

Makes God's Fatherhood Real

Why? Because the Holy Spirit will help to make God's fatherhood – his style of being a father – real. What does that mean? The Holy Spirit will help you to read the Bible and read about God's heart. He will help you to see the truth about God.

When I was a young woman, I was aware of Bible stories and had grown up in the church, but I did not *KNOW* God personally or *KNOW* the Bible. I truly found God through Christ only as a young adult. Then I began to pursue the Bible. At first it was hard. I would pick up the Bible and seek comfort and it would seem to me that I could not find it. But bit by bit, the Holy Spirit worked on my heart and mind. He helped me to understand the stories. He gave me special verses that filled me with hope and courage and patience. I began to see God's love throughout the scriptures. I experienced it more and more. I began to understand the cost of what the Father had done to reach us through the Son, Jesus. I began to see the glorious relationship we can have with the Holy Spirit. Yes, bit by bit, I began to see how God has so many promises for us in His Word, such a great desire to care for His children. Listen to this beautiful opening to Psalm 91 (NKJV):

> He that dwells in the secret place of the most High shall abide under the shadow of the Almighty. I will say of the LORD, He is my refuge and my fortress; My God; in Him will I trust.

A good father protects his children. God is a protector, a defender. That's what Psalm 91 is saying. God is a safe place, a fort, a hiding place where we are protected. He is strong.

A good father teaches and counsels his children. Psalm 32:8 speaks of God's heart to teach us and guide us: "I will instruct you and teach you in the way you should go; I will counsel you with my loving eye on you."

A good father forgives and loves his children. John 3:16 tells us that "God so loved the world that He gave His one and only Son, that whoever believes in him shall not perish but have eternal life."

I could continue with many similar verses that tell us how our perfect heavenly Father fills all the roles of an excellent father as we understand fatherhood. We can't even begin to wrap our minds around all that God is and all that He does.

But let's talk about our identity as God's beloved children.

Makes Our Identity as Beloved Child Real

One of the greatest phrases to hold onto from the Bible is in John 17:23. Jesus is recorded as praying to the Father this request, that "they will see that you love each one of them with the same passionate love that you have for me." (TPT)

This is absolutely a mind-blowing statement that we must not miss. Jesus was saying that the Father has the same love for every one of us as He has for Jesus. 'It can't be so," we think. "I am not good enough. He can't love me like Jesus! I don't deserve that!!"

And you're right and I'm right. We don't deserve it. That is the whole point. God is totally different than we are. We say, "I'll love you if you measure up," and no one ever measures up. Not really. Do they? We get let down and we let others down. But God is love. He does not change. He does not give His love and then snatch it back. He does not give us love based on our performance, but out of the generosity of His great heart. He is love.

The Bible says, "The steadfast love of the LORD never ceases; His mercies never come to an end; they are new every morning; great is Your faithfulness." (Lamentations 3:22-23 ESV)

If we come to understand this, it is a total gamechanger. We stop fighting, being jealous, coveting other people's lives and stuff. We realize God the Father loves us like He loves Jesus, and we can breathe a sigh of relief and rest in His arms. We can be patient. He won't leave us. He will take care of us. Help is on the way. He loves us even when we blow it and fall down. He stays. He stays. He stays. And He sees the best in us that He is working to bring to the surface. God is so, so good.

In closing, I want to pray something the Apostle Paul wrote that is in the Bible. He was writing to a church in a city called Ephesus. Here's what he said, and it is also for you and me:

> When I think of all this, I fall to my knees and pray to the Father, the Creator of everything in heaven and on earth. I pray that from his glorious, unlimited resources he will empower you with inner strength through his Spirit. Then Christ will make his home in your hearts as you trust in him. Your roots will grow down into God's love and keep you strong. And may you have the power to

understand, as all God's people should, how wide, how long, how high, and how deep his love is. May you experience the love of Christ, though it is too great to understand fully. Then you will be made complete with all the fullness of life and power that comes from God. (Ephesians 3:14-19 NLT)

Amen. He loves us. Oh, how He loves us!

Questions for the Small Group Session

1. What memories do you have of your own father or stepfather? Other male relatives?

2. Do these memories make it hard for you to call God father?

3. Why do you think Jesus modelled calling God father for us?

4. If you grew up without a father, would it help to call God father? Would that ease the hole in your heart from your dad's absence?

5. Hebrews 13:5 (NKJV) tells us this: "He Himself has said, "I will never leave you nor forsake you." How can you grow to trust that these words are true? What will help you believe them?

2

Jesus and the Cross

Key Verses

"Christ didn't have any sin. But God made him become sin for us. So we can be made right with God because of what Christ has done for us." (2 Corinthians 5:21 NIrV)

What wondrous love is this, O my soul, O my soul?
What wondrous love is this, O my soul?
What wondrous love is this that caused the Lord of bliss
to bear the dreadful curse for my soul, for my soul,
to bear the dreadful curse for my soul?" - hymn, author
unknown

Issues for the Speaker to Consider

As is true for many people, the addict may be oblivious to the gospel of Jesus Christ. When you gently probe their faith status and ask them about it, their answer may be, "Oh yes, I know about God and I am beginning to trust Him more," but the mix of superstition and vagueness about God doesn't begin to resemble the thinking of a born again, regenerated, and faith filled thinker. It doesn't look like one who knows Jesus personally and KNOWS that he or she has been moved from death to life because of the cross. It is important to note, however, that there are some born again believers who struggle with addiction even after accepting Christ. You may have them in your group too. The issue for them may be a need for growth - for the baptism of the Holy Spirit, the ministry of soul healing, and/or good discipling from mature believers, as well as the healing that comes through treatment programs.

Most all people are drawn to the stories of Jesus' human life, His kindness, His healing ministry. But He was not just an exemplary man. He was God who took on flesh with one overriding mission – to die for the sins of humanity and to restore the identity of "child of God" to each convert. The cross event must be carefully explained. The truth that it was God who "was in Christ reconciling the world to himself," (2 Corinthians 5:19 NLT) must be unpacked in a clear and detailed way. God Himself was hanging on that cross in the form of the Son. That is a concept with which many people struggle whether they are in recovery or not. The notion that God is one, but at the same time, Father, Son, and Holy Spirit, as mentioned in the previous chapter, can be hard to grasp. The idea of God dying for us, in place of us and doing that to spare us, while satisfying justice, is an act of generosity that eludes the average mind, let alone the mind of someone who has rarely, if ever, seen someone trustworthy. And yet, this is the truth that we must get across in language that is simple and makes sense:

"God presented Christ as a sacrifice of atonement through the shedding of His blood – to be received by faith." (Romans 3:25 NIV)

Many have diluted this notion, reduced the voluntary, substitutionary death of Christ on the cross to His offering us simply a moral example of a kind heart. They say, "we are to *copy* His example of unselfishness." Or, they liken His Roman executioners to bullying regimes throughout history that have always annihilated resisting heroes. Jesus' words, "Don't you realize that I could ask my Father for thousands of angels to protect us, and he would send them instantly?" are lost on them (Matthew 26:53 TLB). His death was willingly entered. And they don't understand that He did something for us that could be accomplished in no other way and certainly not by us. Some resist the cross event

> **Many have diluted this notion, reduced the voluntary, substitutionary death of Christ on the cross to His offering us simply a moral example of a kind heart.**

because the concept of the Father offering the Son as a sacrifice for atonement represents reprehensible child abuse to them, so they can't live with that explanation.

They forget that it was, in fact, God hanging on the cross, God as the Son.

The modern interpretation of Christ's death as simply a moral example diminishes the gravity of sin, our hopelessness in removing it from our lives, and the unique capacity that only God possesses to re-right the world from its fallenness. It also negates the depth of the grace and glorious nature of God to fix our situation through being our substitute. *Jesus died to absorb all sin, all sickness, all suffering, and then to offer back to those for whom He died, His resurrected life, His profound love, and power.* His death was a fulfillment of multiple prophecies contained in the Old Testament.

Consider these words:

"[God] chose us in Him (Christ) before the creation of the world to be holy and blameless in his sight." (Ephesians 1:4 NIV)

"He (Christ) is the atoning sacrifice for our sins, and not only for ours but also for the sins of the whole world." (1 John 2:2 NIV)

All the benefits of Jesus Christ's voluntary self-sacrifice can belong to anyone if they will simply trust in Him and receive His work on the cross. It is good news that God did this and takes the lead in giving us a new spirit man and puts His Spirit in us at the time of regeneration and subsequently with greater infilling. We need His power and His grace to navigate this life. A pastor, Samuel Chadwick, once said, "The Christian religion is hopeless without the Holy Ghost."[2] Jesus sends us the Holy Spirit after we have received Him as Savior and Lord and have gone from death to life. He said:

> I speak to you an eternal truth: if you embrace my message and believe in the One who sent me, you will never face condemnation, for in me, you have already passed from the realm of death into the realm of eternal life!" (John 5:24 TPT)

I tell those in recovery who frequently have experienced jail and prison time that, "The warrant was out for us. Our name was on it. Jesus crossed our name out and put His name on the warrant instead. The capital punishment due to us fell on Him and He died willingly in our place." Warrants, arrests, and sentences, many understand! So, the idea of Jesus dying for us and giving us new life begins to take hold.

Pastor Joseph Prince says this in another way, but a way that can be heard by many addicts in recovery: "What is the good news? It is that God loves us so much that He gave His Son to take our beating so that we can have His blessings without having to work for them."[3]

The faultiness of the "moral example" interpretation of the cross is that when we have to follow a good example (Jesus) and try to repeat His actions, we strive for perfection through our efforts and we compete with others to seem better at being good. It is such a puny and destructive interpretation of the cross as compared to the Bible's teaching:

"While we were still sinners, Christ died for us." (Romans 5:8 NIV)

Works righteousness and striving takes us right out of the land of grace and blessing and away from the Christian faith.

"For it was by grace that you have been saved, through faith - and this is not from yourselves, it is the gift of God - not by works so that no one can boast." (Ephesians 2:8-9 NIV)

So, who was Jesus?

This question must be answered fully with many stories of how beautiful our Savior was and is. The healing stories, the teaching stories, the cross and resurrection events - these are all important to unpack. But, because guilt and shame and hopelessness about whether life can be different are hallmarks of the addict's struggle, it is so important to teach the grace involved in Jesus' death and resurrection - that there was a great exchange that occurred on Calvary:

"God made Him who had no sin to become sin for us, so that in Him, we might become the righteousness of God." (2 Corinthians 5:21 NIV)

That righteousness becomes the permanent covering and position of those who sincerely receive Jesus Christ's work on the cross personally. It is for the one who says, "Now, I want to follow Jesus." And along with the forgiveness and clean slate come power from the Holy Spirit who Jesus has sent to us to help us live a Christian life.

Having people give live testimonies of their "before and after" or sharing video testimonies of people's radical transformations through faith in Christ does wonders in stirring up your listeners' faith to believe and receive Christ.

Prayer for the Speaker and The Talk

Father, I pray for this speaker to radiate all the beauty and truth of who Jesus was and is – the darling of heaven, crucified. Since it is true that "if the Son sets you free, you will be free indeed," I pray the freedom from bondage to drugs that Jesus brings for those who will hear this talk. Let love and light and the power of the resurrection pour through this teaching segment. May the joy and peace of a relationship with God through Jesus be so tangible and real. May this speaker stir up such longing in the hearts of the hearers to have ongoing intimacy with Jesus. May every person have faith in Him as their Savior and may they grow "from glory to glory" to resemble Jesus for the world. In Jesus' Name, Amen

"But we all with unveiled face, beholding as in a mirror the glory of the Lord, are being transformed into the same image from glory to glory, just as by the Spirit of the Lord." (2 Cor. 3:18 NKJV)

Sample Talk:

Introduction

What do we need to know about Jesus?

Jesus changed people. Jesus changes people. I have seen this so often in people getting free from drugs. When they find Jesus, they get set free.

I want to tell you one of the testimonies that so changed my life and led me to start helping people in recovery. It is the story of a man lost in drug addiction after having been fairly wealthy. His testimony was presented in a video during a worship service I attended many years ago.

This man traveled with his work and had begun to get involved with drugs at parties in various countries. Soon after, he could not work well, kept getting fired; eventually, he was broke and then homeless, doing drugs out on the streets of New York City.

He had a friend, a woman who was a believer. She kept trying to get him to church. She would even give him a little money, but say, "You have to come to church to get it." At first, he scoffed at God and faith. "It'll never happen," he said. Then as the addiction began to kill him, he became open to God's help. He wound up in a hospital, terribly sick and hearing horrible, mocking voices. Among those voices, however, was one sweet one. From this voice he heard, "The day you call upon the name of

JESUS AND THE ADDICT

the Lord, you will be saved!" Was it the voice of his friend? Was it God? The man called out, "Jesus, help me, Jesus!" and suddenly, the voices stopped.

This was the turning point. The man entered Christian recovery and bit by bit, step by step, he walked out of the nightmare that had been his drug addiction. He accepted Christ. Jesus Christ utterly changed and saved him.[4]

And I might add, Jesus drastically changed me through this man's testimony. From the moment I saw the video, my feet began moving down a new path of loving and helping those who are trapped in addiction. I found myself drawn to people on the street, in shelters, in jail, in transitional communities. Jesus imparted His love and concern to me through this video testimony. He changed me too.

Who was Jesus?

That is power, isn't it? Jesus can take the most hopeless of situations, the most sick, lost, and confused people and put them back in their right minds and give them lives of beauty, dignity, and purpose. Jesus can cause us to want to help others with great generosity, to put others before ourselves and our needs. He takes us to places of ministry that we never imagined.

Oh, He is amazing, this beautiful Savior.

And while He is changing people, He is not shaming them. Do you know the story from the Bible of the woman who was caught in adultery? Yes, the big shots in town somehow caught this woman and found out she was cheating on her husband or the guy she was with was cheating on his wife. Who knows exactly what was going on? That part's not clear, but they dragged her in front of Jesus.

In that day, it said in their law, the Jewish religious law, that people caught in adultery should be put to death by having stones thrown at them. We don't know where the man was who was involved in this. Only the woman, trembling and terrified, was pulled in front of Jesus.

It was a trap, you know. The leaders who grabbed the woman and brought her to Jesus were not so concerned with her sin. They hated Jesus. They were jealous of Him. He was so good, so kind, yet, so powerful, and the people loved Him. The rulers wanted Jesus to say the wrong thing and be made the fool or worse. So, they said to Him, "In the Law, Moses commanded us to stone such women. Now what do you say?" If Jesus said, "Yes, stone her," the people gathered around Him who were looking for mercy and hope would probably desert Him. But, if He said, "Don't follow the Law," there would be reason to accuse Him and perhaps charge Him with a crime.

Jesus, who had been sitting to teach, simply drew in the sand for a moment. Then He stood and said, "If any of you is without sin, let him be the first to throw a stone at her." Then he bent down and began to write on the ground again.

JESUS AND THE ADDICT

One by one, the leaders and teachers of the law dropped their stones and drifted away. They knew Jesus had "read their mail." They all had sins. No one was without them. The woman was left alone with Jesus. He asked her, "Woman, where are they? Has no one condemned you?" She said, "No one, sir." "Then neither do I condemn you," Jesus said. "Go now and leave your life of sin." (John 8:10 -12 NIV)

The gospel books of the Bible (Matthew, Mark, Luke, and John) are filled with stories like this of Jesus healing the bodies and souls of people, leading them out of suffering and sin to new life. To be near Him was and is so splendid. Jesus brings healing, hope, purpose, freedom. He makes all things new for any of us who will take Him into our hearts.

Why did He die?

But, His transformation of people did not stop there. The miracles He performed – healing the blind, the deaf, the lame, lepers, and so on – these miracles are stunning and still go on today – but that was not the greatest thing He did. The greatest thing that He did, that which was His ultimate mission on earth, was to go to the cross and die for all humanity, to save all people.

Death on the cross was a horrible form of torture. Jesus was whipped and tormented beforehand and then placed on the cross. People killed this way would sink because of weakness and pain and then try to push themselves up to gasp for breath. It was grisly and horrible. And it was a death full of shame. That Jesus,

God in the flesh, gave himself up this way for us, is astounding, *1.* but it shows the depth of His love – and it shows how serious the *2.* problem of sin is.

God is a holy God. We cannot be with Him now or in heaven eternally without something being done about our sin. Sinful *1.* people cannot enjoy a relationship with God but saved people *2.* can. That is what Jesus came to do, to help us reconnect to God.

Listen to these words from the book of Titus:

At one time we too acted like fools. We didn't obey God. We were tricked. We were controlled by all kinds of desires and pleasures. We were full of evil. We wanted what belongs to others. People hated us, and we hated one another. But the kindness and love of God our Savior appeared. He saved us. It wasn't because of the good things we had done. It was because of His mercy. He saved us by washing away our sins. We were born again. The Holy Spirit gave us new life. God poured out the Spirit on us freely. That's because of what Jesus Christ our Savior has done. His grace made us right with God. So now we have received the hope of eternal life as God's children. (Titus 3:3-7 NIrV)

What Does That Mean for You and Me?

Let's try to make this even clearer. You know people have always been into trading as a way of each person getting what they want without spending money. My daughter was part of a website community for a while where you could get free stuff. She got a number of things that way. The idea was, people would advertise things they had to give away. They would get things that others were giving away. No money changed hands. People were trading with each other. It was a system of exchange. Free stuff!

At the cross, there was also a trade or exchange that happened. Only this time, it was not an easy or even trade. Jesus, out of infinite love for us and a desire to win us back, took all our sin into Himself. He absorbed all of it. And He also took our sicknesses. "By His stripes we are healed," it says in Isaiah 53:5 (NKJV). For an agonizing moment, He was totally abandoned by the Father as He said, "My God, my God, why have You forsaken me?" (Mark 15:34 NIV) In another place in the Bible, it says that He became cursed for us so that we would not have to bear any curse for our sinfulness. (Galatians 3:13) He got the curse of our sin and we got the blessing God had promised in ages past. We received His pure and holy life, available to us. Let's act it out to make it even clearer.

I have a white cloth and a bag of dirt here. (Doing a demonstration can help the idea of the exchange be better understood.)

Would someone come up here and hold the white cloth? (When a volunteer comes forward, you can continue.) When Jesus died on the cross, what happened was this. Let's imagine this white cloth in _____'s hands is the righteousness of Jesus. _____ is going to be Jesus for us.

What is the righteousness of Jesus? What does that word mean? Well, you might guess that, in part, it means the goodness, the purity, the sinlessness of Jesus. He was without sin, the Bible says. But righteousness also means having a right relationship or good relationship with God. Jesus the Son was in "right relationship" with the Father.

Now, in my hands I have a bag of dirt. I want you to imagine this to be my sin, but even beyond that, the sins of the world, of everybody who's ever lived or will live. At the cross, Jesus took away our sin, the sins of the world. I am going to give our actor the bag of dirt. And at the cross, Jesus made it possible for us to have His righteousness, His loving relationship with the Father. But, I can't have it, this white cloth, unless I give Him the bag of dirt. And I can't have the white cloth unless I say, "Ok, Jesus, I will take from You what only You can give me – total forgiveness, pardon, a new life. I will give you my sins, my repentance, and my life. Will you give me your righteousness, your blessings, your life lived in me?

(Hand the dirt to your volunteer and take the white cloth. If you have a large white cloth, like a towel or tablecloth, this is helpful because you can then wrap it around your shoulders.)

Once I sincerely receive this righteousness, it is a permanent "robe" that I wear. I may still sin and make mistakes, but I remain

42

the "righteousness of God in Christ Jesus." When God looks at me, He sees me clothed with the righteousness of Christ. Now, He is forever mine and I am forever His.

And what about my sins (the bag of dirt)? The scriptures are full of wonderful promises about what God does with our sins when we sincerely repent, choose Jesus, and devote our lives to trying to remain loyal to Him.

Listen to God's kindness to us:

"He has removed our sins from us. He has removed them as far as the east is from the west." (Psalm 103:12 NIrV)

[God says] "I will not remember their sins anymore. I will not remember the evil things they have done." (Hebrews 10:17 NIrV)

(Ask the person playing Jesus to take the bag of dirt and throw it in the trash.) This is what God did with our sins at the cross. That is where *all* His anger against sin was played out. *He is not mad at us.* We need to take hold of this mercy for us and believe that God *chooses* to forget our past.

How Can I Have Jesus in My Life?

You may be saying to yourself, this sounds good. Having my sins forgiven, having a restored relationship with God, getting help to be a good person…I want this. How do I get it?

It is really very simple. You make a decision to follow Jesus Christ. That means you are going to learn as much as you can about what it means to be a Christian. What does a Christian do?

What does a Christian not do? What is right and wrong in the eyes of God? Those will be some of the things that you learn.

But this life all starts with saying yes to the most wonderful Person who ever walked this earth. It just starts with believing and receiving Him. I want to invite anyone who has been considering making a commitment to Jesus to stand up and come forward tonight. We want to pray with you and for you. I am going to invite Jesus into your hearts and pray for you to receive all the help you can get to honor this commitment sincerely. Something very real happens when this prayer is prayed. You may not feel anything physically or emotionally. Simply believe the words of scripture that something very real happens when you follow these instructions: "Say with your mouth 'Jesus is Lord.' Believe in your heart that God raised him from the dead. Then you will be saved." (Romans 10:9 NIrV)

But listen, here's the most important thing. Receiving Christ into your heart by faith means that you are beginning a relationship of love that will grow deeper and deeper as you get to know Him and as you allow Him to touch you with His grace and mercy again and again. The Bible says that Jesus came to earth full of grace and truth. He's going to show you what is true and right. He's going to do it full of grace (helping you in ways you don't deserve). Christianity, at its heart, is simply like the words of the old children's song. It is believing this: "Yes, Jesus loves me. Yes, Jesus loves me. Yes, Jesus loves me. The Bible tells me so."

Come on up. Let's pray.

Note: Here is a sample prayer of conversion:

"Jesus, I have lived my life without You. I have been sinful and rebellious towards God. I want to change now. I believe You died also for me. Please come into my heart and forgive me. Walk with me. Fill me with Your Holy Spirit. I want to be a Christian and serve You and others. Amen"

Never pass up the opportunity to invite people to receive Christ into their hearts by faith. There will always be some who hear your talk who will raise their hand or stand up when you give an invitation to receive Christ. It is not old-fashioned. He is the answer. Offer Him often.

Tell them: After you receive Christ, it is very important to be with people who will help you continue to follow Him. Arrange to be water baptized. Find a good church home with loving (they won't be perfect!) people who believe the Bible, who pray and worship wholeheartedly, who take care of each other, and who reach out to the world with good, unselfish acts. Find a church that honors the Holy Spirit for Jesus promised He would send Him to be with us in this age. He is the power source for ministry. When you find that church which is a good fit, join them, stick with them as best you can unless God leads you on to another. You may have moments of hurt at your church. You will hurt them also, most likely. Learn to forgive and make peace. That's where you'll do it. But continue to grow up into Jesus together.

Continue to grow into more loving people. It's been said, "Be careful who your friends are for you become what they are." Find good, Christian friends so you can all help each other to become like Jesus.

Questions for Small Group Session

1. When you hear or read the stories about Jesus, what attracts you the most to Him? What puzzles you the most about Him?

2. What do you think about the cross? Why did Jesus die?

3. How can a death 2,000+ years ago affect us now? What does it mean to believe in Jesus, to accept His offer of salvation?

4. Many people think they are pretty nice and that that will be enough to get them into heaven. Do you believe in heaven? What do you think it takes to be there?

5. People talk about having a relationship with Jesus. What do you think they mean?

6. What is the difference between the way you've been living and how you really want to live?

3

The Holy Spirit's Power

Key Verses

> "When the Advocate comes, whom I will send to you from the Father – the Spirit of truth who goes out from the Father – he will testify about me." (John 15:26 NIV)

> "But you will receive power when the Holy Spirit comes on you; and you will be my witnesses in Jerusalem, and in all Judea and Samaria, and to the ends of the earth." (Acts 1:8 NIV)

Issues for the Speaker to consider

As previously discussed, theology around the Trinity must be thoughtfully unpacked. Many people, in churches or out of them, addicts and non-addicts alike, have trouble understanding the idea of Three Persons in one God, let alone the character and activities of each Person in the Godhead. As I have said, sometimes the culturally obtained understanding of the Trinity goes something like this: Jesus is a really nice guy, a little short of divinity; the Father is grouchy and has a hair trigger temper, and the Holy Spirit is, well, just strange and better left rarely mentioned because He's not quite understood and perhaps dangerous.

I love a story that English pastor, Nicky Gumbel, has told in his Alpha talks – a newly converted woman, touched by the Holy Spirit, gets very enthused during worship and begins to

> **It's not unusual to go into many a Western church and hear talk about God the Father and Jesus the Son, but have the Holy Spirit rarely mentioned.**

shout "Hallelujah" while standing up. One of the church leaders runs to her to bring her back under tight religious control, saying, "Madam, you mustn't do that here! Please sit down and control yourself!" She replies, "But, I am so excited! I've got religion!" He says, "Well! You didn't get it here!!"[5]

For many, understanding of the Holy Spirit is narrow, shallow or plain absent. It's not unusual to go into many a Western church and hear talk about God the Father and Jesus the Son, but have the Holy Spirit rarely mentioned. You may find this true for the people you are teaching. Perhaps no one has taught them much or helped them experience the Spirit's presence. I often tell people that the depth of my own acquaintance with the Holy Spirit in my growing up years in the mainline church was to hear "in the name of the Father, Son, and the Holy Spirit. Amen. The end. Time for lunch!!"

I am joking, but there was not much teaching about or hunger for the Spirit in the places I grew up. He seemed to be just a part of churchy slogans. The churches I attended as a child were proper and kindly, but very traditional and sedate. We were there to sit still and learn to behave. The Holy Spirit was extremely quenched. Many have had the same kind of Holy Spirit deficit in their upbringing.

On the other hand, sometimes people have had the opposite experience. They have been around places with a more robust desire for the Holy Spirit. But maybe that, too, has not gone so well. Perhaps they had an experience with a Pentecostal church that left them uncomfortable because of its insistence that encounters with the Holy Spirit all look one way. Perhaps people there went overboard trying to manufacture experiences with the Holy Spirit or constantly insisted that a not quite ready member speak in tongues immediately. Having had these sorts of pushy experiences can make people back off settings where they might run into that spiritual discomfort again. God the Spirit becomes linked to human bungling.

You may find people frightened of the Holy Spirit simply because they've heard that experiences with Him can be so powerful and they're a little frightened of a possible loss of control under the Spirit's influence. Though having experienced an extraordinary loss of control through drug use, this spiritual loss of control is still unknown territory. The fear of losing face is a very great fear.

But, let's not get to the matter of power or experiences just yet. Understanding resistance and ignorance are important as we talk about this aspect of our relationship with God, but let's speak first about the basics. Who is the Holy Spirit? What is He like? What does He do?

The Holy Spirit is the third Person of God. He is God. He is equal to Jesus and the Father and is worthy of worship. He is so tender and kind. That is why He is sometimes pictured as a dove. Yet, He is also powerful beyond imagining. And that is why He is sometimes symbolized as fire. He imparts power, teaching, comfort, love, self-discipline, new attitudes, and breaks off unholy habits and sin. He is, as Samuel Chadwick wrote, more than merely the minister of consolation, the "Comforter."

He is Christ without the limitations of the flesh and the material world. He can reveal what Christ could not speak. He has resources of power greater than those Christ could use, and He makes possible greater works than His. He is the Spirit of God, the Spirit of Truth, the

Spirit of Witness, the Spirit of Conviction, the Spirit of Power, the Spirit of Holiness, the Spirit of Life, the Spirit of Adoption, the Spirit of Help, the Spirit of Liberty, the Spirit of Wisdom, the Spirit of Revelation, The Spirit of Promise, the Spirit of Love, the Spirit of Meekness, the Spirit of Sound Mind, the Spirit of Grace, the Spirit of Glory, and the Spirit of Prophecy."[6]

As you can see from Pastor Samuel Chadwick's words above, there are so many dimensions to who the Holy Spirit is and how He can help us. And what Chadwick shared is only a start!

Yes, the Holy Spirit is the source of great power. John the Baptist spoke of Jesus being the one who would baptize us with the Holy Spirit and with fire. These words mean that our Christianity can move to higher and higher levels, more intimacy with God, more experience of God, more capacity to minister like Jesus. The Holy Spirit makes this growth possible. As Jesus promised that we would do "greater things than these, because I am going to the Father," (John 14:12 NIV) and that we would "receive power when the Holy Spirit comes on you," (Acts 1:8 NIV) we are given understanding that there is more to Christianity than just saying the "sinner's prayer," getting saved, and having head knowledge about Christian principles.

There is a life meant for us that would look like Jesus' life. A believer's life is meant to crackle with power and we are meant to see and participate in miracles just as were common in Jesus'

> A believer's life is meant to crackle with power and we are meant to see and participate in miracles just as were common in Jesus' ministry.

ministry. True Christianity is an explosive thing – explosive with love and healing – with experiences. And the Holy Spirit is key to this. As He enters into us, we become enabled supernaturally to significantly affect the world around us. It is this love and power that too often get replaced by rules, self-effort, and judgement as I described in the Introduction. The gospel of Jesus Christ gets buried under manmade religion and religious spirits. Things get very dry. I believe this has been the turn-off for countless people, undoubtedly for many addicts, as they sought help, needed Jesus, but found cold ritual and rejection. Christianity is meant to be relational and powerfully transformative. The Holy Spirit "burns" our brokenness off of us. Many churches know this and live it out, but there are also those who do not.

The Holy Spirit's ministry to us is to draw our attention to Jesus, who also indwells us because of the Spirit, make us to be like Jesus, and fill us with the love, gifts, power, and desire to do the works of Jesus. He carries the works of Jesus out through us.

The truth is, for those who are afraid, any level of power experienced through relationship with the Holy Spirit does not leave us unable to control ourselves. We remain in control. There is no need to fear. Ministering in the Holy Spirit or encountering the Holy Spirit is a little like a surfer riding a wave. We can start moving along in the Spirit's glorious power as we "catch the wave," and then we can pull out as we need to or feel led.

The task for the speaker is to make the character, the work, and the effects on people of the Holy Spirit's indwelling very clear and very appealing. In this age, we are promised that the Holy Spirit will be with us and in us, that He will never leave us (John 14:16). We are told that our "bodies are temples of the Holy Spirit whom [we] have received from God" as believers. (1 Corinthians 6:19 NIV) He is to be our helper, our teacher, our comforter, our guide, our power, our provider of gifts/love for ministry to others (1 Corinthians 12:4-11), our sanctifier, and our deliverer. He is the One who makes Jesus real for us. He glorifies Jesus. He is the kindest Person you will ever meet. He is to be our dearest Friend and yet, He is God. Equal to the Father and the Son. Worthy of equal worship. These things and so much more must come across to your listeners. Prepare to share your own experiences and also get busy with your concordance, searching out everything the Bible would tell you about who the Holy Spirit is, what He does, and how you can have a relationship with Him such that you can pass all this on.

It is the Holy Spirit who enables us to receive Jesus (1 Corinthians 12:1-3) and we are baptized in the Spirit after salvation in order to become witnesses. We also may receive subsequent infillings. The Bible tells us to, "Keep on being filled with the Holy Spirit." This is the true meaning of Ephesians 5:18, that we keep being filled.

As time permits, helping them to understand the joy of giving and receiving healing by the power of the Holy Spirit is a wonderful class exercise. One time, while teaching people in a minimal security facility about the power and the healing gifts of the Holy Spirit, one of the men talked about his hand that had been virtually destroyed by fireworks. He had only numbness in the hand and so would sometimes crush Styrofoam cups filled with coffee, not realizing he was squeezing them very vigorously with his "dead" hand.

I talked with the residents, people trying to recover from addiction, and told them I wanted *them* to minister healing to him. "Let's ask the Holy Spirit for total restoration of movement, all numbness to be gone, a totally restored and working hand."

The people in the class gathered around him and we spoke words of healing in Jesus' name: "numbness be gone, feeling return, fingers move, total healing." I asked him to test the hand and he said, "It doesn't seem different. Thanks anyway! My hand is pretty hopeless." The evening ended.

Not long after this, however, I had an excited message from one of the leaders of the group who told me, "He says he used to wake up with the hand in a tight fist and he would have to struggle to pry it open every morning. He's begun to wake up with his hand loose and open and he's continuing to experience more and more improvement. He is hoping for total healing!"

You must understand that he didn't think anything was going to happen. Half the people gathered around him speaking healing didn't think anything was going to happen. Some were mad at God because of their incarceration, deaths in their families, or because of a variety of things. Some had faint faith, but all of them tried to "give it a shot," and the Holy Spirit, so faithful to us, so powerful, so generous, brought healing into the hopelessness of a hand destroyed by recklessness – through a group made up largely of reluctant skeptics.

We have to understand that *these sorts of powerful events orchestrated by the Holy Spirit often spur people to be open to God where they were not before.* Healing in the Holy Spirit's power should be a central piece of Christian ministry.

> **To know that God is living and can help gives the listeners faith that the scourge of addiction can also be totally removed and that they can remain clean.**

Seeing actual miracles of God's healing and restoration occur raises hope and expectation. To know that God is living and can help gives the listeners faith that the scourge of addiction can also be totally removed and that they can remain clean. There is no better time to share this idea and experience than during the Holy Spirit talk. While getting free of drugs is often a process of healing, it must be said that, at times, the Holy Spirit's sanctification can completely knock out the craving for drugs immediately. The body and mind can be simultaneously delivered from the spirit of addiction and all mental and physical dependencies. I have seen it and heard this testimony given by addicts. "I was completely delivered when the Holy Spirit came upon me."

It is in this age of the Church that He can indwell all of us as we open ourselves to receive. Our bodies are the intended temple for the Holy Spirit in this age. As the fire fell on the altar of the Temple in ancient Israel, so the fire is to fall on the altar in each of our hearts as we are touched and filled by the Spirit. This is a revelation that radically changes individuals, communities, and nations. The Holy Spirit can be *in* us. One minute of true influence by the Holy Spirit on a person in recovery can be worth hours of counseling.

Prayer for the Speaker and the Talk

Holy Spirit, come.

We bless You. We praise You. We thank You for Your presence within us. Yet we know we can experience You more. Come in power, come in glory. We hunger for You to be in us and on us. We hunger for Your manifest presence. Help us, we pray. We need You so much. To be a Christian without Your help is impossible. We long to be baptized in You.

There may be many who listen to this speaker who are unfamiliar with You. Help them to hear the countless ways in which You are present on earth to help us. Help the speaker to teach that we are meant to be temples in which You dwell so that we can be changed from the inside out. Help everyone to realize from this talk, Holy Spirit, that in a minute, You can burn away unholy habits and struggles, making us brand new and so like Jesus.

We welcome You. Come, Holy Spirit. Amen

Sample Talk:

Introduction

Many years ago, I traveled overseas for a meeting of Christian leaders. I had just gone through a tremendously hard season in my ministry. I was feeling down, worn out.

One of the speakers at this meeting got into a conversation with me and said, "You need to talk with _____, and he named another one of the speakers, a man who was quite famous world-wide as a Christian leader.

The first man brought this older, well-known leader to my table. He sat down across from me, pushed the lunch plates to the right and to the left, reached over and grabbed my hands, and said with great gusto, "Let's pray!!"

He had such a twinkle in his eyes. His words came forth with great authority and certainty. Joy seemed to fill him to the brim and overflowing. This man was a man led by the Spirit. He was "dripping" with love and certainty about God. Who could be sad or feel hopeless in his presence?

In that same period of time, I was at a second meeting near my home where another very well-known leader had traveled with some of the worship team members from his church. I wanted to thank him for their leadership in the meetings as so much peace and encouragement had surrounded everything that they spoke or sang.

I saw him by the hostess' counter at the hotel restaurant and went over to say a few brief words. He shook my hand and turned away rather swiftly. I am sure he had much to do. And probably, he often experienced people cornering him to talk. I didn't mind. I started to walk away and that is when IT happened. I felt a great gush of power begin to overcome me physically. Something had poured through him, a great man of prayer, into me.

I hurried to my room as I was starting to feel weak-kneed, like I could hardly walk. Once inside my room, I just stood there trembling with power coursing through me. The experience lasted for many minutes. It was like I had put my finger in the electrical socket of the universe. Something very powerful had been imparted to me from God through the touch of this man. I just stood there, shaking, saying, "Thank you, Jesus," because the presence of God in the room was so palpable and real. I also said, "I'm sorry, Jesus." Why? Because my sad moods in this season were an indication of not really trusting Him. The apostles in the Bible were persecuted and beaten, but their reaction was to rejoice "because they had been counted worthy of suffering disgrace for the Name," the Bible says. (Acts 5:41 NIV) I recognized I needed to renew my trust in God.

When the sensation began to subside, what remained was such joy – I had been touched by God! - and I had a new resolve to overcome the struggles in which I found myself.

Both these stories reflect some of the things the Holy Spirit does. We will talk about them more in a moment, but first, who is the Holy Spirit?

Who is the Holy Spirit?

The answer is simple. He is God.

Like the Father and the Son, the Holy Spirit is God. He is part of the Trinity. He is a Person. God is one, and yet He comes to us as three different people, all of whom are mentioned in the Bible, all of whom are worthy of our devotion and worship.

As Jesus got to the end of His ministry on this earth, He began to tell His followers that "it is for your good that I am going away." "Unless I go away," He said, "the Advocate (another name for the Holy Spirit) will not come to you; but if I go, I will send him to you." (John 16:7 NIV) Advocate means both our Helper and Comforter, but it also means Jesus' representative.

It has been said that the Holy Spirit is like Jesus, but without skin on. He has the same heart but can be everywhere with anyone. In the Old Testament, after reading the story of the Holy Spirit's involvement in creation, mostly there are stories of the

Holy Spirit coming occasionally to a few individuals to help them with particular things they needed to do.

This all changes in the New Testament with the events surrounding Jesus' birth and then following Pentecost, the day of the Holy Spirit filling the disciples. Suddenly, the prophecy given in the book of Joel (Joel 2:28-32 NIV) came to pass – that in this era, the Holy Spirit would be poured out on all people. "Your sons and daughters will prophesy, your old men will dream dreams, your young men will see visions." The Holy Spirit has come in this Church Age and He is available to help us all.

What Does He Do?

In the stories I shared with you about my encounter with two fellow leaders during a time of painful struggle, the Holy Spirit worked through these men in several ways.

1. He kept the first leader who prayed over the lunch table with me filled with joy.

2. He gave him a constant mindset of confidence and rejoicing.

3. He gave him the heart to want to help a stranger.

4. He gave him words of prayer that were right on and helpful.

5. He gave me encouragement and peace through this interaction.

With the second encounter, where I felt <u>physical power</u> flowing through me, the Holy Spirit:

1. Enabled that <u>impartation</u>. Power came from God the Spirit through the leader, whose touch during the handshake imparted power.

2. The Holy Spirit helped me to <u>be aware of God's presence</u> and help through that physical experience.

3. I felt an <u>inner healing</u> of my emotions occur because of that interaction. My mood lifted. I went back into the meetings <u>hopeful</u> and ready to move forward. I was <u>encouraged</u>.

Consider all these things. And this is just a short list! The Holy Spirit heals us whether in body or soul. He makes us aware of God's presence and love. He causes us to want to help each other. He gives encouragement and hope. He touches us with power and causes us to lift our heads up. Oh my goodness, what a dear Friend the Holy Spirit is!

He teaches us about Jesus and reminds us of the words of Jesus. In fact, He is most happy when Jesus is being glorified. He helps us to grow up step by step. But, here is one of the most stunning things. Jesus said, "He is the Spirit of truth. The world cannot accept him, because it neither sees him nor knows him. But you know him, for he lives with you and will be in you." (John 14:17 NIV)

Wow! In us and with us – that is where the Holy Spirit will be.

He Will Be in You

Here is another verse that talks about this truth that the Holy Spirit will be in you:

The Apostle Paul was giving practical advice to the churches he had started which is found in his letters in the New Testament. One of those churches was in a city called Corinth. Paul was telling them not to engage in sexual immorality because our bodies are very precious to God. He said this: "Do you not know that your bodies are temples of the Holy Spirit who is in you, whom you have received from God?" (1 Corinthians 6:19 NIV)

The Holy Spirit can be in you. When you get a hold of that truth, it changes everything. He can come more strongly upon you with more of His manifest presence, but He lives in believers, particularly powerfully in those that have been baptized in the Spirit.

The Baptism of the Holy Spirit

In closing, what does this mean to be "baptized in the Holy Spirit?" Different churches have their various teachings on how this occurs and what it looks like, but let's just look at what is said in the Bible.

When Jesus, at the beginning of His ministry came to his cousin John the Baptist at the River Jordan to be baptized along with all the people there, John was preaching, "I baptize you with water for repentance. But after me comes the one who is more powerful than I, whose sandals I am not worthy to carry. He will baptize you with the Holy Spirit and fire." (Matthew 3:11 NIV)

Jesus would minister full of the Holy Spirit throughout His ministry. The Holy Spirit came upon Him "like a dove," when he was baptized by John, and remained on Him. But the Holy Spirit also enabled Him to minister in power. After His death and resurrection, Jesus instructed His disciples to wait in Jerusalem until they had received the "gift" or the "promise" of the Father. This gift turned out to be the powerful infilling of the Holy Spirit that occurred on the day of Pentecost in Jerusalem (Acts 2). After that filling and subsequent fillings, the inept, sometimes scared disciples became men of power and authority although they were mostly common men, laborers and fishermen. As they preached, the church began to multiply exponentially. The Bible describes the powerful effect they had on people around them. They were arrested by the same men who arranged for Jesus to be crucified and spoke to them boldly about Jesus, the gospel, and the leaders' guilt. The Bible says that when these Jerusalem leaders "saw the courage of Peter and John and realized that they were unschooled, ordinary men, they were astonished, and they took note that these men had been with Jesus." (Acts 4:13 NIV)

How could the disciples do this, knowing they might end up in prison or on crosses themselves? The truth is all but one of Jesus' band of twelve, excluding Judas who killed himself, died martyrs' deaths. But prior to those deaths, they preached and taught, evangelized and carried out astounding healing miracles just like Jesus.

The answer is, "the Holy Spirit living inside of them." The Holy Spirit gave them boldness, power, authority, wisdom, and so many other gifts so that they could spread the good news about Jesus. And it spreads like wildfire even until today.

The Holy Spirit is still filling people today, giving them courage to speak up about Jesus; giving them power to minister healing to others. People are being added to the worldwide Church in amazing numbers, particularly in Asia, Africa, and South America. "In 1900 there were fewer than 9 million Christians in Africa. Now there are more than 541 million." That's just one example of how the Church is growing.[7]

The thing that must be remembered is that much of that growth happens when we act like Jesus for the world around us, when we, filled with the Spirit get the courage to speak boldly, do loving acts, minister healing, pray, and move in power. We need the Holy Spirit. That has always been the way of the Church. We need the Holy Spirit to do anything that resembles Jesus.

Tonight, if you would like to be filled with the Spirit, we want to have a time of ministry for you. In a moment we will invite you forward to pray with the prayer team. (Give them instructions and pray for the group.)

(You may have some leaders there who can be the ones to pray. You may have invited some people from outside your ministry to be a prayer team but allow this time for people to ask God to minister to them. A simple prayer like the one below can be offered. Encourage the person to repeat the words after you.)

"Lord, I know that I need Your strength to live this life and to help others. I would like to be filled with the Holy Spirit. I am asking that from You right now. You have promised that You will give the Holy Spirit to those who ask. Thank You, Father, for hearing me and answering my prayer. In Jesus' Name, I receive the Holy Spirit. Amen" *for your Name sake*

to glorify God the Father
JESUS the Savior

Note:

Tell your people that whether something dramatic or nothing dramatic happens, that their job is simply to put faith in the Bible's words, that if they ask God for the Holy Spirit, He is a good Father who sends Him to us. (Luke 11:11-13)

My own experience of the baptism was a tremendous flow of physical power with speaking in tongues. Certain traditions say this is the evidence of the baptism – speaking in tongues – but there are other differing testimonies from reliable, significant leaders such that we must be gracious in not making rules about what must or will happen. Just prepare your people for possibilities.

Do not skip over this teaching or a time of ministry for receiving the Spirit. The scripture is very clear that a Christian is a

Spirit-filled person: "...if anyone does not have the Spirit of Christ, they do not belong to Christ." (Romans 8:9 NIV)

The Holy Spirit is not just an "option" of Pentecostal churches. He is God. He is for all of us. Let us adore Him and seek Him as such.

Baptism with the Holy Spirit Scriptures:

Gospels: Mt. 3:11, Mk. 1:8, Lk. 3:16, Jn. 1:33; **Acts** 1:5, 1:8, 2:1-4, 8:14-17, 9:10-19, 10:44-48, 19:1-9; **1 Cor.** 12:1-11, 14:1-19

Questions for the Small Group Session

1. How much did you know about the Holy Spirit before you came to this talk?

2. David Wilkerson and Jackie Pullinger are two leaders who found that *praying for the baptism of the Holy Spirit was key in helping people to get free and stay free of drugs.* Does that spur you to find out more about the baptism of the Holy Spirit? Knowing God wants to help you in this special way?

3. Do you believe that a powerful encounter with the Holy Spirit could set *you* free?

4. Do you believe that a powerful encounter with the Holy Spirit could help you to minister the gospel to others? Be bolder?

5. What further questions do you want to ask about the Holy Spirit?

4
Your Identity in Jesus

Key Verses

"Yet to all who did receive him, to those who believed in his name, he gave the right to become children of God." (John 1:12 NIV)

"But you are a chosen people, a royal priesthood, a holy nation, God's special possession, that you may declare the praises of him who called you out of darkness into his wonderful light." (1 Peter 2:9 NIV)

I am no longer a slave to fear,
I am a child of God.
I am a child of God. – No Longer Slaves, Bethel Music,
copyright 2014

Issues for the Speaker to Consider

This is an area where so much concentrated teaching is needed. Many of us do not know what we have in Christ, what we became when we accepted Christ; most especially what God feels about us and towards us. It is because of His own purpose and His love that we are saved. (2 Timothy 1:9) Of course, all of your audience may not have accepted Jesus. Some may be of other faiths. Some, of no faith. This is something you will have to navigate, but don't be shy about presenting the gospel and presenting moments to receive Jesus.

All of Christian scripture is a love letter, it has been said. It points to the revelation of Jesus Christ, hidden in the Old Testament and revealed in the New. The revelation being that God's sovereign plan has been forever to restore us to His side after our immediate and inevitable rebellion against Him. The plan has been marked by a relentless pursuit of us, the ninety-nine sheep being left in the sheepfold while He comes over hill and through valley to find each one and all of us and return us to home, the lost ones. (Luke 15:4-7) He comes not only to deliver us from sin, but to restore the identity intended for us in Creation.

The gospel, simply stated, is that before the "foundation of the world," God had a plan for redemption of humanity. The redemption would occur as an act of total grace from God. There is no plan B. There is no Column A for the Sort of Good, Column B for the Less Good, and Column C for the Total Reprobates. We are all reprobates. "We, all, like sheep have gone astray." (Isaiah 53:6 NIV)

Though humanity was totally fallen - "All have sinned and fall short of the glory of God" (Romans 3:23 NIV), and "the wages of sin is death" (Romans 6:23 NIV), God would make a way for us to be reconciled to Him. It would involve His own bearing of the punishment for our sins as Jesus on the cross. The resurrection would be the vindicating proof that our sins had, in fact, been covered and removed from us by God the Son, and we could now be in the presence of God, restored to Him, found by Him and full of Him.

Through this unilateral action of God, there is the capacity for us to have an identity of beloved co-heirs with Christ (Romans 8:17); once orphans, now fully family members. Once we are in Christ, we are seated spiritually on the throne in the heavenlies with Him (Ephesians 2:6), a people saved by grace, robed in righteousness. We have been granted a new position and new authority, if believers in Jesus.

Many Christ followers do not see themselves like this – absolved of sin and guilt, made innocent again by a God who chooses to throw our sins to the bottom of the sea and forget them. (Micah 2:19) Many strive to earn the Father's love and the salvation already gained by Christ on Calvary. They continue in a mindset of guilt, trying to assuage their consciences with "dead works," (Hebrews 9:14 NKJV) rather than presenting the blood of

Jesus as the only, God-ordained, worthy offering. They work and work, confess and confess the same things, and do not know that after they became a Christian, there is only one identity: beloved, redeemed, pure, spotless, forever child of God. The Apostle Paul wrote, "...if righteousness could be gained through the law (our following rules and rituals), Christ died for nothing!" (Galatians 2:21 NIV)

But, the culture and teaching in many churches lead people to this. "You've accepted Jesus, said the sinner's prayer, now back to work!" In those churches that do not honor the Holy Spirit or believe in a present day miraculous healing ministry of Jesus, this works righteousness can be the norm. I call it the "Martha syndrome." (Luke 10:42)

If you remember, Martha, Mary and Lazarus were siblings and friends of Jesus. At one point, Jesus came to their home in Bethany to socialize. Mary was welcomed at His feet to listen intently to His teaching, to receive from Him. They all were welcome to do this. Mary adored Jesus. She felt loved by Jesus. But Martha worked and muttered and finally complained to Jesus, "I am doing everything, while my sister sits there."

Jesus said, "Mary has chosen the one thing needed and it will not be taken from her." Martha could have received His love, acceptance, and guidance too, but she chose to burden herself with lots of everyday tasks, distraction, and self-effort. Imagine! Jesus was right there in the room with her!

Many Christians lead a life like this anecdote from Martha's life. Jesus is right there in the room with them too, but you would never know it to watch them. They've accepted Jesus as Savior, but, they've gone right back to work, trying to gain God's approval and righteousness by their own efforts as if there had never been a Jesus! In truth, they are still in unbelief and a form of rebellion. They are beset by the spirit of religion.

As stated above, Galatians 2:21 (NIV) explains the folly of this so well: "I do not set aside the grace of God, for if righteousness could be gained through the law, Christ died for nothing!" One Bible commentary contains this comment: "If we can earn salvation by obedience to the Law, then the Cross is redundant."[8]

If we do works out of the identity of being loved and adopted by God, the works are just an overflow of resting in His love for us. The warmth and joy we feel knowing we are His and totally loved by Him pours into the people around us. The works spill out of us as a natural overflow and then onto others. It is empowered by the Holy Spirit in us. We are acting as members of God's household, His heirs. Getting this idea of ourselves, "I have arrived, I am not trying to get there...Jesus did a finished work on Calvary," can be hard. For the addict, it may be doubly, triply hard.

If an addict has come from an abusive home, a life of manipulation,

> If we do works out of the identity of being loved and adopted by God, the works are just an overflow of resting in His love for us.

71

even crime on the streets, their self-image is liable to be extremely poor - even with those who seem full of bravado. This idea of being totally forgiven by grace may be so hard to get a hold of and the idea of being a beloved, *purified* (by Christ's blood) child of God seems out of reach. Their inward thinking may be, "I never got anything for nothing. I had to fight and scrape for everything. I can never be pure. I've lived a life in the gutter. That's who I will always be – damaged. I have such a big stain on me." Their trust in God may be stronger than that which they hold towards other people, but it still may be tentative and easily shaken. Guilt can be a relentless tormentor.

But, with careful explanation of "this is the way God wants it, this is how He did it for all of us – by grace," you can bit by bit draw them into an identity that solely comes out of God's kindness towards them. Fighting the orphan spirit, the sense of lack, the lingering shame – all this is hard. You will have to explain identity in Christ very carefully and more than once.

Additionally, there is some tension between this idea of a new identity and one of the recovery practices that comes from Alcoholics Anonymous. Whereas this program has been the central avenue for getting sober since the 1930's and originally came out of a Christian crucible, the program has evolved from the early days of Bill Wilson and Dr. Bob Smith's Bible studies and Oxford Program connections. The Big Book has much in it that is so in sync with the Bible, but there is a concept from AA that impacts the thinking of recovering addicts which needs to be considered.

People in recovery through AA or other Twelve Step programs are taught to always introduce themselves in meetings this way: "Hello, I'm _____. I am an addict, or I am an alcoholic."

The thought behind those introductions is that the person making them will then not be reckless about their sobriety. They will forever remember what a hold some chemical(s) had on them and they will be appropriately sober-minded about how much it damaged their life and the lives of their loved ones. They are to remain watchful. It's often said that relapse begins weeks before it actually happens. There is a slow slide into it by not being diligent about sobriety, one's thoughts, and behaviors. There is a lot of collective wisdom and experience behind this approach.

But this is, to a degree, contrary to the way Christians are taught to speak of themselves. I recognize that many Christians refer to themselves as still being "a sinner saved by grace." But in truth, that is not correct either. Christianity contains the idea that we were sinners, but if we come to believe in Christ's saving work for us and receive His forgiveness and grace extended from the cross, "we are a new creation." (2 Corinthians 5:17 NIV). In fact, a truly saved person is actually a saint, who remains clothed in Christ's righteousness, even when a fresh failing occurs. Can we still sin? Yes. But our identity is that of "a new creation" and one who is becoming more like Christ every day, from "glory to glory." (2 Corinthians 3:18 NKJV)

Now, I don't deny a healthy and abiding concern for relapse is important, although I think one could make an argument for the possibility that many can receive total deliverance from addiction through divine healing. The need to always be identified with the past is problematic in helping people understand being saved by grace and the possibility of being clothed with Christ. I am "the righteousness of God" in Christ Jesus. (2 Corinthians 5:21 NIV) This is present tense. We gain a new identity or the planned identity since creation is restored. This is the message of the supernatural power of the gospel.

Teaching the new identity of being a child of the King who helps you will challenge you as you face a room of people getting sober, especially if many are poor, are currently incarcerated, or have a prison background. But my experience has been that they often are some of the strongest Christians I have ever known once they realize this.

One last word of caution. As you teach this idea of new identity, this extraordinary, amazing identity we receive in Christ, it is important to remember and convey that sin is still serious. A holy God cannot tolerate sin. That is why He planned the solution Himself, the cross, before the beginning of creation. I find sometimes that teachers and speakers can go overboard on the stressing of God's love without reinforcing the fact that sin remains unacceptable in His eyes. Two of the last places that people allow God to control are their sexuality and their money. And there are countless other places where we can compromise and think, "It's ok if I do this. God loves me." Yes, He does loves us. His love is beyond imagining. But, He loves us enough not to leave us in compromise. Fortunately, the Holy Spirit is constantly speaking conviction, words to spur us to self-examination. I pray that as you teach and feel deep compassion for the heartaches of your audiences in recovery, that you will believe in God enough and believe in the capacity of your listeners enough that you will present this wonderful identity in Christ alongside a continued and even greater push for Biblical purity – consecrated lives. We owe it to the Lord who died for us. He is worthy. Let's give Him the full reward for His suffering. *consecrated = dedicated to God and thus sacred. set apart, clean, holy*

Prayer for the Speaker and the Talk

Holy Father, one of our big challenges is to consistently accept Your idea of us and obediently replace our self-image with it. We struggle to understand that salvation is a free gift. The only work you ask for from us is to believe You. We are so apt, after years of living, to look down on ourselves, and to compare ourselves with others hoping to come out ahead. Secretly though, many of us don't expect to come out ahead in very much, if anything. Help this speaker to have healing of every soul wound regarding their desirability to You and others. Help this speaker to realize their place and position as beloved son or daughter and to speak out of that. Help them to convey to their listeners the possibility of becoming totally convinced of this truth, "I am a beloved child of God." In Jesus' Name, Amen

Sample Talk:

Introduction

Jesus once asked His disciples a question, "Who do people say that I am?" Peter, one of his disciples, was the one who answered the question correctly. He said, "You are the Messiah, the Son of the living God." (Matthew 16:16 NIV) Jesus praised him and said, "This is not a human idea that you have, Peter. That's exactly who I am. You got this straight from my Father in heaven."

Now, I want to ask you a similar question tonight. If someone was to ask you about your identity, how would you talk about yourself? What things would *you* say about yourself? Who are you? Jesus agreed with Peter that He was the Christ, the Messiah, and the Son of the Living God. If you have accepted Jesus into your heart by faith, He is in you. So, how are you talking about yourself these days? Who are you now?

I know, because you are in recovery, many of you would say, "I am a recovering drug addict." Maybe some of you would also describe the job you have, where you came from or whether you have a family or not. You would give some facts about what's going on in your life and about your past.

Those things are all part of where you've been, who you are, and what you do with your time. But, I want to dig into something deeper tonight. I want you to think about who you are once you've accepted Jesus Christ as the Savior, Healer and Transformer of your life. If you have done this, what things can you say to describe yourself as you walk with Jesus? And if you haven't taken this step, think about what changes receiving Jesus *could* make in your identity.

Jesus Makes us Children of God

Let's consider this idea. When you receive Jesus Christ into your heart by faith you become part of the family of God. You become God's child. John wrote in his gospel, "Yet to all who did receive him (Jesus), to those who believed in his name, he gave the right to become children of God." (John 1:12 NIV)

What does that mean to be a child, not a servant, a guest, or an outsider, but a child who belongs to someone? In a good home, when you are one of the children, you sit at the table, you eat the meals with the family, you share in the family's income, you receive affection, the family name. You feel accepted. You feel secure. We could list many things, in a good home, that you receive by being a member of the family. Now think higher for a moment, if this is true of a good human home, what about being a child in God's family? Can we say the same things? Yes, you have the family name, you share in God's provisions and the wealth of heaven, you have intimacy with the Father, you have security from Him, communication from Him, and so on and so on. Being His child totally transforms your life and brings many blessings with it. Do you have to earn this? Can you earn this status? No, you are born into it when you are born again spiritually through Jesus Christ. You receive all these benefits by simply believing in Jesus.

We Receive New Names and Callings

With the new identity you gain, you receive new names. The "righteousness of God" in Christ Jesus, may be the most important of all these names. (2 Corinthians 5:21 NIV) This means that when we accept Christ as Savior, what He did on the cross works for us. Our sins were forgiven at the cross and we receive that benefit. All that was broken in us has been absorbed by Christ and all His righteousness is put on us. We are permanently clothed in His "robe of righteousness," once we accept Jesus. That means that we now have nothing standing between us and God. Jesus has taken it all away so that we can be close to God and build our relationship with Him. The old, rotten stuff about us is gone, and the new has come. We are covered by Jesus' identity. It has become ours.

We have other new names and descriptions. Peter wrote about Christians that we are "a chosen people, a royal priesthood, a holy nation, God's special possession, that you may declare the praises of him who called you out of darkness into his wonderful light." (1 Peter 2:9 NIV)

Imagine this, that God sees us as a chosen people, a royal priesthood, and a holy nation. What do these thoughts mean? Aren't only a few people priests and pastors? That sounds like it is something beyond us, perhaps.

What Peter was saying with these words is that we, once we receive Jesus, are all called to worship and love God, to minister to Him like priests in the temple of our hearts. We are called to share who God is and how we found Him through Christ. We are to be people who "declare the praises of him," that is, we're meant to share our stories and testimonies of how God saved our lives. We are meant to tell others about this "wonderful light," where love, joy, peace, patience, kindness, goodness, faithfulness, gentleness, and self-control, the fruit of the Spirit reign in people's hearts including ours. We're meant to change the world – not just the professional pastors but all people who are following Jesus. We're meant to change it by our beautiful and winsome speech and by our loving acts. "They will know we are Christians by our love," the song says.[9] Our new identity given to us by Christ, helps us to do this.

We're also meant to change the world by our boldness and courage. Many Christians face incredible persecution around the world. They are killed, or family members are killed, their property stolen, homes and church buildings burned. To speak up about Jesus Christ in many places can earn you a death sentence. Yet, the Holy Spirit in them gives them boldness and commitment to speak up.

There was a very dedicated pastor named Richard Wurmbrand who stood up against communist leaders in the 1940s in his country of Romania. For his courage, he received imprisonment. He was held fourteen years for simply being a Christian who would not compromise with the godless government of his country. He wrote a book that is widely read, *Tortured for Christ*. In it he spoke about the prison guards and their horrible treatment of him and other Christians. He said, "We preached, and they beat us. We were happy preaching; they were happy beating us – so everyone was happy."[10] Actually, far worse was done to him and many Christians in the Communist prisons. His account of the torture is almost beyond readable, it was so horrible. When he came out, he founded an organization called the Voice of the Martyrs. This organization exists to aid Christians everywhere who are being persecuted yet who keep on witnessing for Christ. Yes, we gain commitment, boldness, and the ability to love enemies as part of this new identity. It is an amazing level of super-human strength that comes from God.

We Gain New Abilities and Gifts

The writers of the Bible described spiritual gifts in different books (1 Corinthians 12:4-11, Romans 12:6-8, Ephesians 4:11-13, for example). We can summarize gifts and abilities from God by just saying this: When we receive Jesus into our hearts by faith, the Holy Spirit comes to live in us. We can be filled with more of the Spirit on later occasions, but what He does for us is make us more like Jesus.

We become people who can preach, minister healing, understand scripture better, do acts of kindness, hear God's voice in dreams and visions, lead others to Christ, and so on. We become able to do ministry, in other words. This is the new identity that God gives us.

Many times, I have shared the story of seeing Chinese people being baptized outside in a bathtub in a snow-covered, obviously very cold region. I saw this on a video shared by a missionary couple from that area which they would not name specifically in order to protect the people there. They explained to those of us attending the meeting that these people were brand new Christians. As soon as they were baptized, their goal was to travel westward across the old "silk road," (trading road in ancient times) and go lead many people in the Middle East to know and love Jesus. They came up out of that tub with the rosiest cheeks and a look of shock from the freezing water. Then, off they went, to be traveling evangelists, as brand-new Christians.

This is the new identity God gives us – freedom to do things in His name based on His gifts and directions for us. We are immediately part of the family, spreading its love. Yes, there are things to learn, wisdom to gain. But you are immediately welcome to share the gospel, give your testimony, minister to others, and help them transform their lives. God imparts abilities and wisdom supernaturally as well as through our study. But, we can begin to build His family with what we know at the moment and continue to grow as we walk forward in this new life.

We Are Citizens of Heaven

One last thought about our identity: The Apostle Paul wrote that we are not really citizens of this earth. We are really citizens of heaven, once we receive Jesus. That means that the things everyone else is chasing after – things that break and rust, things that cause us to fight with each other – should not be the goals of Christians. We're living for eternity. We're guided by the goals and values of heaven, love and mercy, truth, justice, hope, and kindness to the most hopeless and poor.

Paul wrote that there are "many who walk along the Christian road" who are "really enemies of the cross of Christ. Their future is eternal loss, for their god is their appetite: they are proud of what they should be ashamed of; and all they think about is this life here on earth. But our homeland is in heaven, where our Savior, the Lord Jesus Christ is..." (Philippians 3:18-20 TLB) He was saying that we must avoid being compromised Christians, Christians in name only, who chase after earthly goals like those who don't even know Jesus. I am not saying that God does not want us to prosper here. He does. He wants to bless His children with good health, a sound mind, and have us prosper in all we do. (3 John 1:2), but we need to be fixed on the long-term strategies of heaven.

The new identity that the Holy Spirit shapes in us as He keeps our hearts and minds on Jesus is an identity that is not selfish, greedy, or unholy. It is not an attitude of competition and shoving others aside. No, it is an attitude of goodness and having a mind like Christ increasingly with each passing day as we keep our eyes on Him and grow in resemblance to Him. It's an attitude that causes us to put the needs of others ahead of our own. We hunger to see all people come to faith and we work for that. We seek to please God above all else.

This is the new identity in Jesus that you may have already, or you can receive. Once you are a believer this is how God sees you. He sees the image of Christ on you. The past is blotted out, gone away as if it never happened. You are a new creation in Christ. You have new things to do as a part of the family of God and you are loved and secure as part of God's family.

Yes, you may sin and do something that doesn't agree with what being a Christian is all about. The thing to do when that happens is simply to say, "Father, I have sinned. I am truly sorry. I want to start over. Help me." You will not have lost your position as a child of God covered with Jesus' righteousness. God will simply help you to get back up, correct your mistake, and keep walking with Him into the future.

Questions for the Small Group Session

1. How did you feel about yourself growing up? Compared to your brothers and sisters? Other kids? Your parents?

2. How do you honestly see yourself now?

3. What do you do when you feel ashamed or burdened with guilt? When you feel anxious or downcast? Is your self-esteem on a roller coaster?

4. How can you gain God's acceptance? (discuss salvation) And how can you be sure you have God's acceptance now, that it is not something you have to earn and re-earn? (discuss assurance of faith)

5. Read Proverbs 29:25-26 (NIV)
"Fear of man will prove to be a snare, but whoever trusts in the Lord is kept safe.
Many seek an audience with a ruler
But it is from the LORD that one gets justice."
Do you find yourself seeking to earn the approval of other people constantly? What traps do you get into because of that? How could you learn to live differently?

5

Thinking in a Brand New Way

Key Verses

"As a man thinks, so is he." (paraphrased from Proverbs 23:7)

"Do not conform to the pattern of this world but be transformed by the renewing of your mind. Then you will be able to test and approve what God's will is – his good, pleasing, and perfect will." (Romans 12:2 NIV)

Issues for the Speaker to Consider

The Bible tells us that "by one sacrifice he (God) has made perfect forever those who are being made holy." (Hebrews 10:14 NIV) What does this mean?

It means that for those who receive Jesus as Savior, who respond to His forgiveness with repentance and willingness to follow Him, their spirit is made alive, regenerated. At salvation, the spirit, the innermost part of our being, is made perfect forever by the Holy Spirit leading us to Jesus and effectually changing that part of us. Now, we can relate to God, Spirit to spirit.

We are beings who consist of a mind, a body, and a spirit. In the act of salvation, Jesus, the perfect, one-time sacrificial Lamb of God, makes possible for our spirits to be perfectly remade. God said, "I will put a new spirit in you...and I will put my Spirit in you..." (Ezekiel 36:26-27 NIV)

> In the new spirit given to me, I have a work of God in me. In God's Spirit given, I have God Himself - a living Person - to dwell with me...The Holy Spirit renews that innermost self, and then dwells in it and fills it. And so, He becomes to me what He was to Jesus, the very life of my personality. Let me bow in holy silence and reverence to say: My Father, I thank You that Your Holy Spirit dwells in me, in my very self.[11]

We were at 0 without Christ, dead, but with Christ, we are 100% remade in our spirits. They are renewed, made perfect by the Lord. We go from dead to eternally alive.

But, and this is a very important - our minds and bodies are not perfect yet. There may be healing needed in our bodies and our minds are "in kindergarten," so to speak, spiritually.

Many addicted people have a level of maturity that froze when they began to delve into drugs and alcohol. "I began using drugs at 16," says the recovering meth addict who is now 32 years old but thinks and reasons as a 16-year-old for the moment. Their mind stopped going forward at that time that the drugs took over.

> **Many addicted people have a level of maturity that froze when they began to delve into drugs and alcohol.**

Additionally, because of the use of alcohol or drugs to fill the void inside reserved for God's presence, there may be a great spiritual immaturity, a lack of knowledge about God, but also a lack of ability to process many events and emotions with spiritual wisdom and insight. The person in recovery needs help to correct immature thinking, faulty coping behaviors, selfish thoughts, self-hating thoughts, and so much else in their minds. There is a great deal of growing up that may need to occur.

What are some of the poor thinking behaviors that may be the addict's standard way of reacting? Dr. Stanton E. Samenow is a psychiatrist who has done a great deal of work with men and women in prison. He understands the criminal mind very well. Because of his work, much has been made known about this defective type of thinking. He has helped so many people to move from broken thinking into healthy, responsible thinking. What he has discovered is also useful in working with many addicts – not just those who have done jail and prison time, and many have that in their background, but for understanding the addicted mindset.

There can be similarities. The recovering addict may, at first, be full of self-pity and an unwillingness to take responsibility for their actions. After all, they often have been mistreated, so they are sad and feel they have a right to feel sad, look out for themselves above all others, and feel resentment. There may be a tendency to give up easily, to want things right away, to struggle with others for power and place, and to avoid having to be responsible and grown-up.[12]

There may be a desire not to lose face, to want others to feel uncomfortable or less powerful than them. There may be a tendency to lie or at least shade the truth. When sad, the temptation may be there to use drugs. When happy, the temptation may be there to use drugs. There is certainly a lot of shame and guilt and sadness to work through. There are memories of abuse and pain. There is fear. Realizing that emotions come and go and can be worked through is a new viewpoint. Developing Biblical thinking that consists of trusting God constantly, loving one's neighbor, being pure, scrupulously honest, putting others first, showing generosity, reshaping one's thinking by scripture, and letting faith and beliefs lead emotions, all these ways of being a Christian responding to the world, may be new.

But everyone's story is slightly different. That must always be remembered. Perhaps there are those in your audience with a faith background who entered into drug use after a devastating tragedy. They may be listening too. But, because of the tragedy and their response to it, the healing of their thinking and memories is also needed.

Our minds are the place where so many battles go on between healthy, redeemed thinking and distorted, defective thinking.

So, teaching the idea that the mind must be renewed and then demonstrating how to do that with God's help is one of the more challenging lessons we have to present. And this must be talked about often - "your thinking needs to change." As thinking changes and beliefs change, behavior changes. Emotions can be shaped and controlled. They can follow the lead set by our redeemed thinking.

Just a word here. Addiction is spoken of as a disease today, not as a moral failure. This is helpful because once the addiction is in place, it does control the body, neural pathways, ability to choose behaviors. Genetic contribution to becoming addicted is always being explored. And yet, we still have to press the classic ideas of sinning against God vs. obedience to God. Sobriety is obedience. If the idea of *choosing* to follow God is not put into the conversations around recovery, the addict can feel hopeless to change. "I have a disease. I cannot control it or be freed from it." There needs to be an appropriate balance between sympathy and urging the person in recovery to do the "next right thing." "You do have choices and you can walk out of this disfiguring way of life into wholeness and peace." A sense of the ability to have control over circumstances must be transmitted along with your compassion for your audience. This is actually honoring them.

There is another element to the changing of thought and that is dealing with "soul wounds." One of the most excellent Christian teachers of soul healing in this era is Katie Souza. Katie, herself, was a drug user and seller, as well as a prison inmate. But Jesus Christ delivered her. Filled with the Holy Spirit, she has become a powerful and renowned Christian leader who is a superb teacher of how to heal the soul in order to become a robust, believing Christian.

> There is another element to the changing of thought and that is dealing with "soul wounds."

Katie teaches that soul wounds occur as a result of "our own sin, someone else's sin toward us, through trauma, and through generational iniquities, things passed down through our family."[13] A soul wound is a way of perceiving the world that is defective. We have been hurt so we respond out of that hurt, often not even realizing that our perceptions and reactions to the world are skewed. Katie has written that:

"A wounded soul affects every single area of your life. It can:

- Cause you to think wrong thoughts.

- Impact your will, causing you to make wrong decisions.

- Cause you to feel painful, negative, hurtful emotions."[14]

An example of this is a woman I met on an overseas ministry trip years ago. To others on the trip, she appeared to be extraordinarily confident, navigating her way around the foreign country we were in with great expertise. She seemed to be able to handle every new experience with more ease than anyone else. She was a whiz in the marketplace getting tremendous bargains, haggling prices way down. She spoke of being able to do the same thing back home. The rest of the ministry team watched her in action and said, "Wow! Wish I could do that!" But one quiet afternoon, when we were resting in the mission house and she and I were the only two roommates left in our room, she asked, "Do you think people like me?" I was startled. What an odd question from such a "together" woman. "Why do you ask that?" I said.

She began to tell me that she could only get so close to people and then "a button would get pushed," and she would start to retreat on the inside, pulling away internally, protecting herself. She described a childhood of abuse and an adulthood of broken relationships. It became clear that the confidence that we thought we perceived was a strong coat of armor keeping her from being hurt yet again. She had some gaping soul wounds of rejection, fear of abandonment and loss that needed the healing power of Jesus' death and resurrection to touch. Those wounds needed identification and then ministry. They needed to be washed by the blood of Jesus and the redirection of His word applied to them. Otherwise, she was doomed to continue this life of strutting about with her head held high fooling everyone that she was bold when inside, she was "dying," desperately lonely and rigidly stuck in dysfunction.

Soul healing is a critical part of overall healing in addiction recovery. We have powerful weapons in the blood of Jesus and the cross's effects, Holy Spirit power, and the renewing of the mind through the Word of God. We have a powerful weapon in the application of healing prayer. Helping people see that sometimes when they think the worst of other's motives, or they get offended and angry, or find themselves weepy and dejected; all these "moods" may be from the distorted thinking that comes out of soul wounds and/or can be from demonic influence. When they begin to understand this, they will be redeemed from thinking, "Man, that's just the way I am...I wish I could control it, but I can't. It just comes over me." They will move to thinking, "Wow! I am getting free from those old reactions. My emotions are going to become consistently stable. I can get through difficult circumstances without collapsing or relapsing. I can identify the devil's tricks of entering my thinking through my wounds to torment me. I can think in a more logical and mature way. I am a brand-new creation in Christ. Praise God!!! And I am emotionally stable, constantly trusting God."

One of the big helps we can give to people in recovery who, understandably, feel beaten down is the ability to reframe things, to see "the glass half full, not half empty." Cheering people up and helping them to see the "bright side," is a great privilege and a holy calling.

Prayer for the Speaker and the Talk

Father, in the name of Jesus,

Help this speaker to give powerful examples of distorted thinking displayed next to wonderful testimonies of healed thinking. Help them to use humor and tenderness to open the hearts of the listeners to this most important topic. Changed thinking changes everything. When we can see the distortions in our mind up against healed, Christian mindsets, hope enters our picture. Help this speaker to be firm about the need for healthy thinking. It is easy to be destructively sympathetic, not requiring much out of those listening. But we will truly love them when we say, "You CAN change your thinking and you must change your thinking." Help this speaker to present the unvarnished truth of Your Word. Help them to speak the words of Jesus, "Neither do I condemn you, BUT, go and sin no more." In Jesus' Name, Amen

Sample Talk:

Introduction

We've got one simple Bible verse for tonight. It is Proverbs 23:7. It says this: "As a man thinks, so is he." What does that mean? It means that what is going on in your brain will determine how you feel, your decisions, and your emotions. Your thought life is very important. What you think about and what you believe in is like the engine on a train. Everything else falls in behind your thoughts and beliefs. Like cars on a train, your emotions, attitudes, decisions, mood, behavior, all get pulled along by this engine - what you are thinking.

If your thoughts are dark, self-pitying or resentful, for example, how are you going to be feeling and talking and acting? Not very well, right? Thoughts like that lead to a chip on the shoulder and bad decision making.

If we're going to get really healed, we have to talk about and learn about thoughts and how to change them. We have to learn the skill of reframing our thoughts to help us cope better with what we are experiencing. People tend to look at the world somewhere between two different extremes - as an optimist (a happy, positive thinker) or as a pessimist (a sour, everything's wrong with the world type of thinker).

There is a sermon illustration that's been shared more than once, but it makes the point about positive versus negative thinking. The story goes like this: Two boys, twin brothers, were exactly the opposite in their attitudes. One boy was so optimistic, so cheerful, his parents worried that he might get really hurt one day by some difficult situation that he didn't see coming. On the other hand, his brother was so pessimistic, he never looked for the bright side of life.

The parents took the boys to a doctor who said, "I can help them both get a better, more balanced view of the world." He put the pessimistic boy in a room full of toys and he took the optimistic boy to an area with only horse manure and a shovel.

As they watched the boys without them knowing it, the pessimistic one sat frowning in the corner of his room saying, "I don't have anybody to play with." As they went to look at the optimistic boy, they saw him happily digging through the horse manure. "What are you doing?" the doctor asked him, stunned to see him so happy. The boy answered that with all the horse manure around him, he was just sure there had to be a pony in there somewhere.[15]

It is a silly story, but it reflects how many of us think. For a lot of people, the only thing seen are the problems and the downside and out of those thoughts comes grumbling, complaining, despair, irritation, and anger. Like the little boy in the room full of toys, we just can't see anything good about our situation.

Others have learned to think differently. They see things that may be difficult or unpleasant and they find a way to still feel good and have positive emotions. They're happy when things are happy, but they also can be upbeat even when things are hard. The key is how you think about things and what kind of interpretation you put on what you see. Once you've chosen to think about something a certain way, your emotions will follow. If you are having negative thoughts, darker emotions will follow, as well as behavior that may not be the best.

If, on the other hand, you have learned to see things in a good light, and I would add a faith influenced light, your emotions and behavior will be far more positive. Having an attitude of gratitude certainly helps you to see things in a more positive light too. If you believe God is with you and helping you at all times, and you thank Him, your thinking will become consistently positive.

We've got to learn to do some really excellent thinking.

Spirit, Soul and Body

Let me explain something about how God made us.

You and I are made up of three parts. We consist of a body, a soul, and a spirit. Sometimes, people use the words soul and spirit to mean the same thing, that invisible part of ourselves that is eternal and that interacts with God. I want to change your thinking on that a little tonight. Soul and spirit actually represent two different parts of us.

Let me give you a scripture that helps us to understand this. The apostle Paul wrote this blessing: "May your whole spirit, soul, and body be kept blameless at the coming of our Lord Jesus Christ. (1 Thessalonians 5:23 NIV) There is a word for spirit and a separate word for soul used in this passage. Soul, therefore, can be used to mean a part of us separate from the spirit. It can be used to speak of our mind, will, and emotions – that thinking and feeling part of us.

Why is this important to know?

An Immature Mind

It is important because of what happens to us when we are saved by Jesus Christ. When we ask Christ into our hearts by faith, we do not just go from "being bad to being a little better." We go from being "dead" to being "alive." Jesus said,

> Very truly I tell you, whoever hears my word and believes him who sent me has eternal life and will not be judged but has crossed over from death to life. (John 5:24 NIV)

When we come to faith in Christ, our spirit is made perfect. Life is breathed into this part of us and our spirit is 100% redeemed. That inner part of ourselves is totally perfected, brand new. Here is verse that explains this: "For by that one offering (Christ's death on the cross), he made forever perfect in the sight of God all those whom he is making holy." (Hebrews 10:14 TLB)

How can you be perfect forever in one part of you and still be in the process of being made holy? Well, here's the answer. Our spirit, that very inner part of us, is made perfect, but our soul needs some work. Remember, your soul is your mind, will, and emotions, the thinking part of you.

Let me put it even more simply. When Jesus saves your life, your spirit graduates from college, so to speak, but your soul or your brain is still in kindergarten! You need to grow more in the way you think, in your attitudes, in the way that you respond to the world. You need to grow up in your mind. So, to repeat, at salvation, you have a perfect spirit! But your brain or soul is still in kindergarten. We have to work on our thinking and change it for good.

Growing up in Mind

How do you do this? How do you grow up in your mind? "I am the way I am," you might say.

First, you have to come to acceptance of the idea that maybe your thinking isn't just what it needs to be. You have to come to the realization, "I may need to change my thoughts for my life to go better." Maybe you will say, "I have too many jealous thoughts." Maybe you will say, "I have too many angry thoughts." Perhaps it's too many thoughts of, "Poor me." Or, maybe you have thoughts of giving up and quitting too easily. You know what goes on inside of you. Maybe you have a hard time just yet catching all your faulty thinking, but some of it, I will bet, you recognize.

You know some of what goes on in your head and whether your thoughts are leading to good emotions and actions or not. It might be that, at first, you need people who are a little ahead of you in their recovery to point out to you when you are off track. They will be able to point it out for you. It will take a lot of humility to receive that. But sometimes other people can see where you are off track better than you can. As you grow, however, you'll get better and better at catching it yourself saying,

"Now that was foolish thinking! Why did I let myself see things *that* way?"

One of the reasons you let yourself "think that way," is because your soul is wounded. In the past, when you did wrong things, when others did wrong things to you, and because, perhaps, of wrong things passed down in your family, you may have wounds in your soul. You look out at the world through those wounds. Your perception is distorted. The wounds need to be healed. And the healing is not that hard. It is a process of applying the healing of Jesus through prayer and scripture to where you have been hurt.

The Bible gives us some very specific words about working on our thinking. Here's one place, Romans 12:2 (NIrV):

Don't live the way this world lives. Let your way of thinking be completely changed. Then you will be able to test what God wants for you. And you will agree that what he wants is right. His plan is good and pleasing and perfect.

Do you hear that? God tells us to avoid living the way many in the world live. He is telling us not to relate to other people the way much of the world relates. He wants our thinking to be completely changed. He wants us to see that He loves us and has our best interests in His heart. He wants us to see that His innocent and pure ways are the best ways even though the whole world may mock them as foolish. Living a decent life, making good choices, controlling our negative emotions, forgiving and getting along with others is the way to go so that life has value and peace.

Emotions Following Healed Thoughts

We can learn how to think well by studying the Bible and memorizing passages that particularly "speak" to us. There are always more mature people around, sponsors, Christian leaders, and people who can be mentors who can help you to change your thinking. The Big Book and other Twelve Step literature give such good guidance on changing your attitudes and thoughts. And certainly, praying, asking God for His help to change your thinking is the most brilliant of steps to take. "Everyone who calls upon the Lord will be saved." (Romans 10:13 NIV) "Saved" covers many things, including gaining a better thought life as the Holy Spirit helps and teaches you. (Psalm 32:8)

As stated before, our emotions get born out of our thoughts. What we think about then gives rise to emotions good or bad. For instance, if I am thinking, "Everyone mistreats me," my emotions will then be full of a lot of sadness and self-pity or a lot of anger. If the thoughts can be made more specific, you can move out of these moods. Let's say you are having problems with only one or two people, but you've made that a broad thing, saying "everyone." If you can correct your thoughts and take out the exaggeration, you will be much better off. Then you begin to focus. You say, "It's not everyone with whom I am having a problem. It's only this person or these two people." Then if you can reflect on why you are having problems and think about how you can work through them with those one or two people, there's no need for dramatic emotions or heavy moods. You are on your way to solving the problem in some way with clear, focused thinking that's accurate.

Good emotions follow healed, maturing thinking. It is so important to renew our minds, as the Bible says. Practicing gratitude daily is so important in terms of having good thinking. If we are thankful and see what we have already, it is very hard to be a grumbler!

Questions for the Small Group Session

1. Do you have a thought/thoughts that continually come up that don't feel comfortable? For example, feeling mistreated, wanting to escape from difficult situations, feeling overwhelmed?

2. Are you able to calm yourself down? Talk yourself out of worries or wound up emotions? How do you do it?

3. If you're struggling with thoughts or emotions, who do you turn to for help in re-framing how you are seeing things?

4. What kind of person do you feel most comfortable being around? Why do you think that is?

5. What kind of person makes you most uncomfortable? (Might be someone very strong and outgoing. Or, it could be someone very quiet. Or, someone that reminds you of a difficult relationship in the past.) How can you learn to be more comfortable with this type of person?

6. In what way would you like to grow more in the next six months?

6

No More Triggers: "I've Got the Devil's Number"

Key Verses

"Now the serpent was more crafty than any of the wild animals the LORD God had made. He said to the woman, 'Did God really say, 'You must not eat from any tree in the garden?'" (Genesis 3:1 NIV)

"Adam was but human. This explains it all. He did not want the apple for the apple's sake, he wanted it only because it was forbidden. The mistake was in not forbidding the serpent; then he would have eaten the serpent."[16]

Issues for the Speaker to Consider

One of the quickest roadways out of recovery is romance.

I don't know how many times I have seen this. Someone starts to feel good about their sobriety. They have been clean several months. They have gotten a job. Things are starting to work for them. But they look around the recovery community and spot Romeo or Juliet a few seats away, and suddenly their high and lofty goals get more earthbound. "If only I had someone to 'love.'"

Nothing derails a good season of sobriety faster than making another human being the new drug of choice. Hormones are relentless hecklers.

> **The devil is prowling like a lion, constantly looking for the weak one to cull out from the herd to tear to shreds.**

Just because the addict makes the decision to finally "work the program," and come in off the street, just because he or she hears a little about Jesus doesn't make temptation less of a reality for him or her. It is part of life. Scripture, in fact, warns us:

> Be alert and of sober mind. *Your enemy the devil prowls around like a roaring lion looking for someone to devour.* Resist him, standing firm in the faith, because you know that the family of believers throughout the world is undergoing the same kind of sufferings. (1 Peter 5:8-9 NIV, italics added)

The devil is prowling like a lion, constantly looking for the weak one to cull out from the herd to tear to shreds. He does not cease this constant activity to take us out, to find the weak entryway into the soul of his targets. Even Jesus, after enduring forty days of fasting and severe testing by satan, leaves the wilderness full of the power of the Spirit, but with these haunting words hanging over Him:

"When the devil had finished all this tempting, he left him (Jesus) until an opportune time." (Luke 4:13 NIV)

In other words, just when you have a great victory over severe testing, is exactly when the next test can begin. It must be taught that "you cannot let your guard down." This is not to say that we don't get stronger and more able to resist the temptations, triggers, and tests of the world as we mature in the faith. It doesn't mean we are not protected by God. We do have increasing victory and ability to spot a strategy of the enemy as we grow in the wisdom of God, but the point is, the devil *doesn't let up*. After he's had someone addicted, out on the streets, committing crimes and being half crazy, is he happy when they become a decent, sober, God-fearing Christ-follower?

No, he's furious.

And he's clever. Remember the Apostle Paul's words, "for Satan himself masquerades as an angel of light." (2 Corinthians 11:14 NIV) He is saying that something can enter your life that looks delightful or innocent or even like a promotion, but it might still be a bit of cleverness of the devil to get us back off track, distracted from God.

In a small church we served a number of years ago, several recovering addicts began to join, becoming part of the community. There was a young couple with a child who had had a rocky relationship, but under the influence of the church, they began to change. They had been through more than one session of detox, inpatient treatment, and outpatient therapy intermixed with relapses, but at this point, they really seemed serious about "getting it right."

And they seemed to want to make their relationship solid. No more on again, off again, leaving their child in chaos. They wanted to get married and build a home. We felt sure this time they meant it. So, the church went all out on creating a beautiful outdoor wedding for them. A flower covered trellis, decorated chairs, music on loud speakers, a wedding cake, wedding clothes, gifts for their apartment – they were treated like a son and a daughter. It was a beautiful wedding, and everything seemed perfect. The church even purchased a night at a hotel for them to celebrate.

But that is where the downfall began. They went to the hotel and decided together that a wedding wasn't a wedding without a toast to their marriage and since they had been sober for so long, "one drink wouldn't hurt them. After all, that's how every tv movie they had ever seen about a wedding had unfolded." But, "even satan comes disguised as an angel of light." That toast did hurt them. Others might be able to drink a toast, but not them.

The moment they bought the wine coolers and began to share them was the moment that a colossal relapse that had probably been simmering for weeks began full steam ahead. It resulted in all sorts of disaster and ultimately, down the road, in their final and permanent break up.

They had not reckoned with the fact that temptation is really real. That celebrations can contain triggers for relapse just as sorrows and stressful situations can. The devil DOES prowl around and look for a way to take us down. We have to be aware and put up safeguards, call on others to help us hold ourselves accountable, and constantly lead a life of "entering (and re-entering) by the narrow gate." (Matthew 7:13)

Our church felt an extreme sense of chagrin and responsibility over this experience. We should have known better and thought about the potential for even a good experience to be a source of undoing for them. We needed to bear in mind the power of temptation. Human kindness is so good, but it needs to be mixed with godly wisdom and with firmness based on awareness of the realities of evil and temptation. Otherwise, WE participate in helping people to be taken down by our softness.

What needs to be taught more thoroughly in the Christian community is that there is evil. It does oppose all that is of God and we need to be mindful and prepared. Evil will whisper doubt and compromise and the promise of delight – anything to get us to choose something less than what God has planned for us which may take discipline and sacrifice.

The contemporary Western church does a grave disservice to people by trying to explain every reference to the demonic in the Bible as "an old-fashioned term from quaint people in the past, saying, 'we don't talk or believe that way anymore.'" The Holy Spirit who inspired the writers of scripture is God. He is omniscient, omnipotent, omnipresent, eternal. He is not catching up to all of us modern folk with our "vast insight" and psychology degrees.

Many a contemporary church leader, at least in the West, goes out of their way to substitute "mental illness" or "epilepsy" or some other term for those passages where Jesus or the disciples encounter and deliver someone from an evil spirit. Yes, there is mental illness that is a specific entity. It is also described in the Bible. But there is also that which is described as demonic or spirit driven because it was real then. And still is. If we understand that the world has not changed, we'll be able to prepare for the ways in which we are tempted and tormented by the enemy of our souls. We will have our battle armor on, be prayerful, and not fall prey to the tricks of the enemy be they subtle or highly dramatic.

> The chief battle, of course, is to maintain consistent faith in our hearts and resist the tactics of the enemy to steal it.

It is important to teach what is called spiritual warfare, being aware of the invisible world and attacks upon us that emanate from it. The chief battle, of course, is to maintain consistent faith in our hearts and resist the tactics of the enemy to steal it. That is not to say that we attribute every negative thing to demonic forces. Some people go way overboard in this opposite direction, but we need to have the balance of belief with trust in God's greater strength.

Many who resist developing a theology of evil are fine with belief in a good God, the history of Jesus' life, death, and resurrection, the belief that Jesus saves, and the idea of going to heaven after death. If you press them, they would have to admit these concepts have to be accepted by faith. After all, much that forms their benevolent concepts is invisible too. They have never seen Jesus in the flesh, nor have they been in heaven. Yet, they accept these things by faith. Perhaps, they are even comfortable with the notion of angels being unseen helpers who minister to the saints. (Hebrews 1:14)

So, why then, are they uncomfortable with accepting the concept of other spiritual forces in opposition to God also being real. Many scripture passages speak of this realm:

For our struggle is not against flesh and blood, but against the rulers, against the authorities, against the powers of this dark world and against the spiritual forces of evil in the heavenly realms. (Ephesians 6:12 NIV)

Certain behaviors, for example, dabbling in fortune telling, horoscopes, palm reading, tarot cards, etc. open people to an unseen and dangerous realm. Drugs, themselves, open people to demonic influence.

Being influenced by "spiritual forces in the heavenly realm" is to be guarded against, but we also can come under attack by other people being influenced by evil. As one's life comes into sync with what is godly and biblical, other people, who are in rebellion against God, may find all kinds of ways to attack or at least, try to persuade, the person seeking holiness to abandon it. Many who choose Jesus can come under attack from friends, co-workers, even family, trying to loosen one's hold on the new Christian life. This is part of the "warfare," staying steadfast, accepting attack and at times, loneliness, as you repeatedly choose the right path.

Jesus told His followers life might look like a series of battles:

"Remember what I told you: 'A servant is not greater than his master.' If they persecuted me, they will persecute you also. If they obeyed my teaching, they will obey yours also." (John 15:20 NIV)

"I have told you these things, so that in me you may have peace. In this world you will have trouble. But take heart! I have overcome the world." (John 16:33 NIV)

Prayer for the Speaker and the Talk

Father, help this speaker to present this information with courage, biblical foundation, and thoroughness. Let no fear of people cause the speaker to gloss over these topics or lessen the deadliness of sin. Arming one's self, praying and worshipping in order to be clothed in Your strength and presence is critical for navigating life. For those escaping addiction, understanding the ferocity of the enemy and his desire to steal, kill, and destroy is so important. But, just so, realizing his defeat at the cross and the far greater strength of You, our Savior, is more important and is the life-giving truth. Help the speaker to present this cosmic battle, presenting the end from the beginning, that You have overcome the world and that all we need to do is to cling to You, to love You, and follow You with our whole heart in order to succeed in this world and enter an eternity to be spent with You. In Jesus' Name, Amen

Sample Talk:

Introduction

Let's start by reading some verses from the book of Genesis:

Now the serpent was more crafty than any of the wild animals the LORD God had made. He said to the woman, "Did God really say, 'You must not eat from any tree in the garden?'"

The woman said to the serpent, "We may eat fruit from the trees in the garden, but God did say, 'You may not eat fruit from the tree in the middle of the garden, and you must not touch it, or you will die.'"

"You will not certainly die," the serpent said to the woman. "For God knows that when you eat from it, your eyes will be opened, and you will be like God, knowing good and evil." (Genesis 3:1-5 NIV)

Some of you may know this story very well. For others, it may be brand new. In a moment, we will talk about it and unpack this conversation that was going on between a serpent and a woman called Eve.

Tonight, our purpose is to talk about keeping ourselves safe from acting on temptations.

You all know very well the concept of triggers. These are things that you encounter that might draw you back into addiction. You have learned or are learning how to spot those things and to avoid them or handle them with wisdom.

But, let's talk about triggers in a biblical way in this session. The Bible has another word for "triggers," and it is temptation. One definition of temptation is that it is a "solicitation to that which is evil."[17] In other words, temptation is an invitation to do wrong – to do something that is not in God's will.

A trigger is a form of temptation. It is an invitation to go back into a harmful, old, way of life. And if it is an invitation, then this means that behind something that triggers you to go back to drugs or to do something else that hurts you or others, is *someone* doing the inviting. You may think, "Oh, it's just me and my thoughts that are starting to take me down the wrong path," and you might be right. You may need to just catch yourself in these thoughts and say, "This needs correcting," and then get yourself back on the right path.

But, I want to suggest to you tonight, that often behind the triggers and the temptations is a force of evil. The Bible refers to this enemy as satan or the devil. Like God, he has plans for your life, although they are not plans to give you hope and a future. Hope and a future are God's desire for you (Jeremiah 29:11). Satan's plan, on the contrary, is to kill, steal, and destroy – you. He has *no other plan* than this. (John 10:10) He wants to take you out.

I should pause here and say people have various opinions about the personal nature of evil. Some people say there is no such thing as satan or spirits. Others see a demon behind every bush. Somewhere in between these two ways of viewing the world is a healthy, balanced outlook. It says, "Yes there are forces of evil, but no, they are not responsible for everything. And God is far stronger than this band of rebels." Nevertheless, if you begin to study the Bible on this topic, satan and forces of evil, you will find many mentions of it, especially in the New Testament. You will also be able to protect yourself and pray far more accurately about difficult things in your life.

So let's hear a little more from the Bible on the nature of satan and his helpers.

The Apostle Paul wrote about them in this way. He said:

Last of all I want to remind you that your strength must come from the Lord's mighty power within you. Put on all of God's armor so that you will be able to stand safe against the strategies and tricks of Satan. For we are not fighting against people made of flesh and blood, but against persons without bodies – evil rulers of the unseen world, those mighty satanic beings and great evil princes of darkness who rule this world; and against huge numbers of wicked spirits in the spirit world. So use every piece of God's armor to resist the enemy whenever he attacks, and when it is all over, you will still be standing up. (Ephesians 6:10-13 TLB)

Paul spoke of the "strategies and tricks of satan." Other translations talk about the "schemes of satan." You know that if a team can get its hands on the playbook of the opposing team (though that would not be fair), they might much more easily win a game. If a general could learn the battle plan of the opposing general before the fight begins, he might be much more likely to win the battle or even the war.

We need to understand that there is an enemy of God and of us and it will help us greatly if we know his strategies and are prepared before he launches an attack.

I knew a young woman on probation, trying to get her life straight after addiction, jail, and criminal activity. One day, I was giving her a ride and she said to me, "You know, I used to have thousands of dollars in my lap as a regular thing. I had a boyfriend who was a dealer and I helped him with it. When I walked down the street, I could see that people had fear and respect for me. I was tough."

"That all sounds pretty fulfilling on the surface," I said. "Money, a relationship, people's respect or at least, fear. Then what happened?"

"I lost everything," she said. "Even weight. I got down to skin and bones. Ninety pounds! The police arrested us. I lost my kids. Many of the things in our house that we had bought with the money were confiscated. I went to jail, got on probation. I now have nothing."

"So," I said, "If you have a moment when you think, 'those were the good old days, I'd like them back,' what do you do with that temptation?"

"I just play the tape to the end and I have no desire to do the things that got me that ending," she said.

That is a phrase I have heard from more than one person in recovery, "I play the tape to the end."

As we think about handling triggers and avoiding temptation, one of our first defenses is to remember "how did it go last time when I gave into this thing?" Play the tape to the end. That will often be enough to stop going down a familiar road of failure.

But let's think of some more safeguards to stay protected from bad choices.

In the Bible story we read tonight, the serpent/satan was tempting Eve by saying a few things he always does. When you think about ways you have been tempted to do wrong, you may see how this story connects to your experiences.

Satan is Crafty

If you've got a weak spot, satan will find it. It's like picking the right lure when you're after fish.

We used to take our kids fishing when they were small. We had this one lure that looked like a shiny little silver fish. It had two hooks on it. As soon as you cast it, a fish would "strike," almost before it hit the water. Even our (at that time) four-year-old daughter was pulling in fish right and left and sometimes catching two at a time. With this perfect lure, we were fishing like pros.

Satan knows the lure for you. He knows where you are growing strong and he knows where you still are weak. He will provide the lures to draw you into trouble through those weaknesses. Eve wanted more even though God had given her and Adam a whole garden, His company, and permission to do about anything they wished, but eat from one tree in the center of the garden. She wanted more. Her thinking was flawed and she lacked gratitude.

Satan Tempts us to Doubt God

The serpent began to work on Eve by stirring doubt in her mind about God's goodness and the nature of His instructions. He said to Eve, "Are you sure God said…" This was the effort to cloud her thinking and make it hard for her to remember. He wanted to make her go back and forth in her mind. "Did He say this or did He say that?"

Then satan said, "Are you sure God said you cannot eat of any tree in the garden?" Well, this, of course, was not God's instruction at all. He did not say no trees were allowed. They were able to eat of all trees, except for one. There was only one forbidden tree out of an entire garden. Satan plants doubt in our minds about God's goodness and God's instructions. Satan insinuated that God did not wish them also to be wise and to discern between good and evil. He planted the seed of suspicion that God was keeping something from them. He made it seem that life was of much less quality without eating from this tree. His temptation was in this form – seeds of discontent, quietly planted. "You're being cheated," he was whispering.

Satan Tempts us to Forget What We've Got

In the moment of her interaction with the serpent and in her desire to have more – the serpent had said, "You'll be like God, knowing good and evil," the serpent was saying to her and he says to us, "If you do things God's way, your world will be too limited. If you go the direction I am pointing out, you'll have more freedom, power, knowledge, wealth, fun" – whatever satan is waving in front of you as a temptation at the time.

But Adam and Eve had so much in God. The beautiful garden. All the animals. Intimacy. Authority. The only thing they had to do to be obedient was to stay away from <u>one</u> tree. Just one.

How many times are our lives like this? When we really think about where we are and what God has done for us, we'll see friendships, safety, maturity, new opportunities, joy, good experiences, faith; so much that God has given us or restored to us. And if we're patient, prayerful, and focused on God's goodness, we'll also see what is coming down the road has the potential for being better. But satan wants us disgruntled and complaining, failing to see all that the Lord has done. He wants us to forget our identity as God's people and God's identity as Provider, Promise Keeper, Savior, and so on.

Satan Downplays the Outcome

Eve said the penalty for eating from the forbidden tree would be death. But the serpent in a wily voice said, "You will not surely die." This is why it is so important to understand the supernatural nature of and the one behind temptation. The devil wants us to think there is no bad outcome if we follow him – only gain.

But just like my young friend said about loving a dope dealer and participating in his business, when she played "the tape" to the end, she had no desire to go back to this form of making what had been a lot of money. Her desire was to find some other way to be secure. She began to work on her GED and to take other steps to start growing and becoming more capable of earning a living.

The devil does not want us to think of the guilt and the losses that will come with listening to his voice and acting on it.

We've got to begin to recognize more quickly and fully when it is his voice.

If we're hearing words that tear us down, make us feel oppressed, gloomy, and miserable, chances are he is stirring that emotion up. We can "growl" back at him, "In the name of Jesus, be gone. I am not listening."

If what we hear are words of invitation to do something we know is wrong with the accompanying thought of, "This is no big deal. Everybody does it. No one will notice. You've been working hard, you deserve a break, you deserve *this*," or similar justifying words, chances are that is the devil too.

Keep measuring all that you hear in your mind by these two questions, "Does this sound like God? Or does this sound like the evil one?"

If you hear yourself accused and put down and therefore, you are tempted to do something wrong to build yourself up, chances are it is the enemy's voice. With practice, you can begin to tell when satan has returned to try to trip you up once again.

Let's close this tonight by hearing the rest of what the Apostle Paul wrote in Ephesians 6 as the way to protect ourselves from the devil's lures:

> So use every piece of God's armor to resist the enemy whenever he attacks, and when it is all over, you will still be standing up. But to do this, you will need the strong belt of truth, and the breastplate of God's approval. Wear shoes that are able to speed you on as you preach the Good News of peace with God. In every battle you will need faith as your shield to stop the fiery arrows aimed at you by Satan. And you will need the helmet of salvation and the sword of the Spirit – which is the Word of God. Pray all the time. (Ephesians 6:13-18 TLB)

Next time you're furious or weepy, or you find your mind lingering on doing something you know you shouldn't, think, "Is this my idea or am I receiving an engraved invitation to trouble?" You're going to get sharper at spotting satan dangling something in front of you and you're going to stop "biting."

Then pray and praise God like everything depends upon it, because it does. There is no greater escape route than to begin to praise and worship God. You will become lost in the Lord and be immune to the devil's tricks. "Submit yourselves, then, to God. Resist the devil, and he will flee from you." (James 4:7 NIV)

Questions for the Small Group Session

1. How much have you thought about the source of evil in this world? Does it make sense that there is an "intelligence" behind it? That people can be tricked and manipulated by it?

2. There are words in scripture about satan "prompting, tempting, and then entering Judas (Jesus' betrayer)" ...and then "It was night." (Beginning at John 13:2) Does it make sense that the more we give into evil, the more it has a hold on us?

3. What teaching have you experienced about the demonic in your past? Does this make sense to you? What questions do you have now?

4. Scripture says that Jesus defeated satan and his troops at the cross, "And having disarmed the powers and authorities, he made a public spectacle of them, triumphing over them by the cross." (Colossians 2:15 NIV) Why then, do you think, we can still be bothered by evil forces?

5. In the talk, you heard that one of our greatest escape routes out of the oppression and discouragement of "the enemy" is to begin to praise God. Have you tried this? Is it working as a strategy of escape for you?

7

Putting Holy Habits in Place

Key Verses

Therefore, everyone who hears these words of mine and puts them into practice is like a wise man who built his house on the rock. The rain came down, the streams rose, and the winds blew and beat against that house; yet it did not fall, because it had its foundation on the rock. But everyone who hears these words of mine and does not put them into practice is like a foolish man who built his house on sand. The rain came down, the streams rose, and the winds blew and beat against that house, and it fell with a great crash. (Matthew 7:24-27 NIV)

"As iron sharpens iron, so one person sharpens another." Proverbs 27:!7

Issues for the Speaker to Consider

One of the last instructions Jesus gave to His small circle of devoted disciples was to go and make other disciples. Matthew 28:18-20 (NIV) describes this scene:

> Then Jesus came to them and said, "All authority in heaven and on earth has been given to me. Therefore go and make disciples of all nations, baptizing them in the name of the Father and of the Son and of the Holy Spirit, and teaching them to obey everything I have commanded you. And surely, I am with you always, to the very end of the age."

One of the primary things we are to learn how to do as a Christian is to be a disciple of Jesus and then help others to do the same. One dictionary definition of disciple is "a convinced adherent of a school or individual."[18]

In Jesus' day, disciples would attach themselves to very learned rabbis, following them everywhere, imitating their ways, serving them, and hanging on to their teachings about scripture as supremely authoritative. A total commitment and attachment was gladly given to very competent and recognized rabbis. The rabbis would disciple their followers. In various scriptures we see Jesus addressed as "Teacher" or "Rabbi." It is this same sense of total commitment and attachment that is still meant today when we say, "We must become disciples of Jesus Christ." Our lives must be totally wrapped around the One we are following, every area surrendered to His guidance.

The beautiful difference between adhering to an ancient rabbi and believing in Jesus is that then, people were admiring a human being, trying to imitate him via their own strength and growing skill. Those who choose Jesus are trying to obey and follow too, but they get filled with divine presence and are given Holy Spirit empowerment. Those who choose Jesus and seek to follow Him are not doing this in their own strength! They learn from where the power to succeed emanates and they seek it. True presentation of the gospel presents these wonderful truths of Christian discipleship again and again:

> **You can keep this divine connection up through prayer, worship, Bible study, and fellowship with other like-minded people.**

You choose Jesus. Your sins are forgiven and your slate is made clean. The Holy Spirit comes to fill you. Christ is in you because of the indwelling Spirit. The Spirit will constantly help you to remember Jesus' words and He will fill you with divine presence and power to carry out those teachings. You can keep this divine connection up through prayer, worship, Bible study, and fellowship with other like-minded people. This is not YOU trying to be good. You become a new creation. And you have the life of Christ being formed in and lived out through you with divine empowerment.

This is the awesome reality that can be found by people who give their lives to Christ. They are no longer struggling to do things by gritting their teeth. They have heavenly aid.

One of the primary things we need to share is how to do this, how to become a disciple of Jesus and remain a fervent one. If we can teach people in recovery a new way of life, that of Christian discipleship, and help them practice and take root in it, they will have the best chance of succeeding in sobriety.

The problem I see across the Christian landscape, especially when it comes to a person who is in recovery and who is a new follower of Christ, there is not nearly enough support and teaching about the experiential nature of Christianity and about what it means to become like Christ. The idea that discipleship is a daily choice and the "means of grace" must be used daily is new. This practicing of faith, putting Jesus' words into action, must be stressed.

What are the means of grace? These are ways in which we stay connected to God in order to constantly experience have His presence, power, love, instruction, and guidance. They are also ways, in turn, that we spread His presence and power wherever we have influence. They include practices like prayer, fasting, studying the scriptures, worshipping, being baptized, receiving communion, spending time with the Christian community, and doing compassionate acts.

I have seen too many people flounder in their recovery and go back to old behaviors because they had only gotten as far as conceding that "Jesus is a good guy," and "I ought to be like Him." They get stuck somewhere between their original vague notion of God – "He exists" - and a fuzzy, primitive understanding of Jesus. "I'm supposed to say the sinner's prayer and then try to be good." They don't develop a robust, intimate relationship with Jesus nurtured by private devotional time which is the next step. Perhaps, no one has taught or modeled for them *and through His Word* that you can really know God through the Holy Spirit. You can hear His voice through the scriptures, worship, dreams, visions, etc. This "stuff" is really real. And in order to "resist the devil," you must "submit," or totally give your life to God and the ways of God (James 4:7). Every day must be a new day of getting up and saying, "Here's my life, Lord." Lord may seem like an old-fashioned, perhaps hokey word to some, but the sense of it is "God is leading me, and my life is totally surrendered to Him." This mindset about God's leadership is a source of safety as we don't have one foot in God's territory and one foot in worldliness. That casualness and its dangers comes from lack of reverence for God.

As I have said, the problem with this very tenuous connection to Christ that is sometimes the situation of a new Christian in recovery is that as soon as pressure comes, old behaviors can set in. Without being *established* in faith, it is easy to start slipping backwards.

A sage jail official once said it to me this way. "Suppose you are right-handed and someone tells you, 'No, from now on, you need to be left-handed.' This is the way it is for someone who has known a criminal or an addicted lifestyle or both. When they attempt to walk away from that, it can feel strange. They're having to switch from something they know to something that feels so new and sometimes awkward. It will all be fine if there is no trouble in their life and they have plenty of ease to use that awkward 'left hand.' But let pressure begin and it's easy to quickly revert back to what they've always known." He was, of course, talking about those incarcerated in his jail who were learning new life skills having enough time to practice them and enough mentoring to help them make a solid transition. Without a lot of practice and support, they could fail easily. If something would go wrong in their lives after just being released, say an unexpected bill, or a job loss, very quickly they could revert to illegal activities because that is what they had always known. *know Jesus*

We must understand the necessity of good, invested discipling of people in every community, but especially with those who are trying to escape the multi-faceted "jail cell" of addiction. People who have been addicted have been prisoners in mind and body. If someone has also had the experience of breaking the law to fund their addiction and being incarcerated, they have a lot of need for help to reform their goals, their hearts, and their lives. Accepting Jesus Christ and being filled with the Holy Spirit bursts open the "jail doors" but next, good teaching and support in how to make discipleship their walk in this world is critically needed. Love and loyalty to them, firm teaching mixed with tremendous compassion, these are the things that will help the Christian lifestyle to be appropriated. Discipling takes time and it is vitally important.

What does a disciple of Christ look like?

The central, primary core belief of a disciple of Christ is that Jesus Christ is God. He is Savior, Redeemer, and Lord. He is God who became incarnate for the sake of a sinful and rebellious world. The only way to be reconciled and in renewed, right relationship with God is to receive Christ into our hearts by faith as our personal Savior; as the one who forgave us at the cross and gave us new life through His resurrection. Jesus is not an option and He is not simply a "great teacher" or a "fully self-actualized human being." True Christianity presents Jesus as God, fully human, but fully divine. We come to believe that we must surrender our lives to Him for transformation in us to occur.

The initial step in discipleship, then, is surrender. You cannot find life as it was intended, on your own. You need help. You need what only God can do for you. And God has done it in a particular way. He absorbed our sin and brokenness into Himself as Jesus on the cross. All that awaits is for us to grasp that He loved us that much to lift our burdens off of us. It has been accomplished in the

> **The central, primary core belief of a disciple of Christ is that Jesus Christ is God.**

supernatural. Now, we need to receive it in the natural. We need to say, "Thank You, Jesus. I accept what You have done." Like the ancient disciples, we need to attach ourselves to the One whose ways are above all others – to Jesus Christ.

In the Bible, it is stated that Jesus "is the atoning sacrifice for our sins, and not only for ours but also for the sins of the whole world." (1 John 2:2 NIV) He is declared the Savior of the whole world whether received by the world or not.

Repentance is part of this first step to a Christian life. It is the response to becoming aware of a holy God. We recognize that there is something basically wrong with us. We see that, as would be disciples, we must be different from the world around us. We realize that we have partaken way too much of the world. The way we are to act and relate to others cannot conform to the world's ways any longer. We say, "I'm sorry, forgive me." We receive the forgiveness that took place at the cross. We turn and fix our eyes on Jesus, saying, "Now, how shall I live?"

Where before the "non-disciple" may have thought of his or her own needs first and primarily, the disciple of Jesus is one who puts the needs of others before himself. Where the world may have counseled "Look out for number 1 because no one else will!" as the smart way to navigate life, Christian discipleship leads us to share, care, and humbly put others before ourselves.

Christianity is full of one another phrases: "love one another," "forgive one another." "Forgive one another as the Father has forgiven you." For example, from scripture, we hear:

Be kind and compassionate to one another, forgiving each other, just as in Christ God forgave you. Follow God's example, therefore, as dearly loved children. (Ephesians 4:32-5:1 NIV)

This "forgive one another," in the Christian faith is radical as will be discussed in a later chapter. We are not only to forgive small infractions from reasonable people, but to forgive heinous enemies, those who persecute us.

God asks us to carry the message of freedom through Christ to the world. Discipleship must cause us to reach out and help others. "By this everyone will know that you are my disciples, that you love another." (John 13:35 NIV) Our calling as followers of Jesus is to help others with our time, talents, and money. We are to do acts of mercy as a regular way of life. We are to carry Jesus and therefore, the miraculous, out into the world, ministering healing, telling the story of Jesus, and giving our testimonies of how He loved and freed us. This is a prime principle of Christianity, that we must "share the good news of Christ and our own liberation through Him." We cannot be silent. In fact, Jesus, in His final instructions to His disciples told them to go and wait in Jerusalem for an empowerment that would come to them making them able to verbally and through lifestyle, share their faith in Christ. He said that their waiting and receiving of the baptism of the Holy Spirit would do the following for them:

> ...you will receive power when the Holy Spirit comes on you; and you will be my witnesses in Jerusalem, and in all Judea and Samaria, and to the ends of the earth. (Acts 1:8 NIV)

One of the hardest things for people to do can be to share their faith vocally. To be open and bold about who they are in Christ and tell others how they got to this place, what they were before, and what Christ has done for them. Many people say, "But people will know I am a Christian by my love, by my good deeds." Certainly, they will be able to spot that "something's different" by unusual acts of kindness and service, but we need to be able to speak up and share what it is to be "saved by Jesus." We need to witness at the appropriate moments when prompted by the Holy Spirit. We need to be able to speak of sin and salvation and other aspects of the faith. We don't help people by leaving them where they are without an opportunity to know and choose Jesus. So, a strong component of Christian discipleship is to tell others about the Christian life and the One at the center of it, Jesus. Being able to do this is dependent upon a relationship with the Holy Spirit. Without Him, we are often weak and frightened.

Along with witnessing verbally, is ministering like Jesus. This is a part of the Christian lifestyle and is promised by Jesus.

Very truly I tell you, whoever believes in me will do the works I have been doing, and they will do even greater things than these because I am going to the Father. (John 14:12 NIV)

Filled with the Holy Spirit, disciples can minister healing to fellow believers and non-believers alike and have an expectation to see miracles. Many non-believers are more receptive to healing prayer than believers! And people in recovery must be encouraged to believe that the Holy Spirit will work through them in this ministry of healing like Jesus. His enablement is not just reserved for those who have led circumspect lives. The reason is that none of us has led a circumspect life! We have "all sinned and fall short of the glory of God!" (Romans 3:23 NIV) But many addicts feel an especially strong unworthiness. You must help them, through this and other talks to realize, God is the only One who is worthy. We are not. We, all, in one form or another have rebelled. But He is full of grace and love for people, wanting us all back and choosing to work through every one of us, despite our flaws.

One of my favorite illustrations of this is one night at a recovery meeting where the talk that night had been on the healing ministry, I asked my small group meeting afterwards, "Does anyone have a health issue that needs prayer? Let's not just hear about healing. Let's do it!" One of the women said she had a sore ankle, injured in an accident and it was giving her problems at her job where she had to stand on it for long hours. She said there was metal in her ankle inserted during surgery.

I asked the group of people in recovery, some who had been incarcerated, to minister healing – short phrases like "pain be gone; bone, muscles and ligaments be strengthened in Jesus' name, etc." They gathered round her, some new at faith, some more experienced, all having the addiction/recovery experience in common, a few put their hands on her and they ministered healing. At the end of this healing ministry session, we threw in "and metal be gone!"

A couple of weeks later, I was back with the group and asked her, "Is your ankle better?" She said, "Why yes, it is," and as she answered she rested that ankle on her knee and began to touch it almost to confirm her own report. Suddenly, she gasped, "I can't feel the metal anymore!!" It was delightful. She was so stunned by her own miraculous discovery, she couldn't say much for a quite a while afterwards. Many months later, I had a message online from her.

"I'm still healed!" she said. "This is building my faith way up!"

The point is, God works through all of us. We do NOT qualify ourselves for this. He qualifies us!!! And there is nothing more delightful than seeing someone who was far from Him becoming one of His greatest advocates and spokespeople. Discipleship is important! Helping people learn the many dimensions of being a

Christian, praising their fledgling efforts, backing up the principles with scripture, and teaching them more is so important. Teaching them to teach others will also be important. And having them stay rooted in this new life is the goal.

A big part of discipleship is to join a community of disciples, that is, a church - which is not a building, we should remember, but a body of people - and grow with them. It is important to worship, pray, and study scripture, alone in regular times of personal devotion as previously mentioned. But it is so important to also do these things with others, and to be around people with greater wisdom, experience, and maturity, if possible.

Church communities are never perfect. In them are people in all states of their own "recovery" from sin. There are people with various unhealed soul wounds. And so, you have potential for offense and strife. We must enter our church communities with the idea that "as far as it depends on [me, I will] live at peace with everyone." (Romans 12:18 NIV) "I will be a peacemaker, not a peace breaker." One learns the skills of forgiveness and compassion only by being with people not by being a loner.

Though there are many more things you can teach in this lesson about discipleship, probably Jesus' admonition to "take up your cross daily and follow me," will be a most important one to include. It sometimes comes as a surprise that becoming a Christian does not automatically remove you from all the difficulties of life. But to a struggling, recovering addict, perhaps someone with large court costs, working at an entry level job, with health issues left over from the addiction, setbacks can become a real "dark night of the soul" moment. "Why, oh why, God, have you forsaken me?" can be the understandable heart cry when the going gets tough.

Helping people recovering from addiction to grasp the idea of meaning-filled suffering, of holding onto faith even during duress will be a great challenge. In their past, many would just get high or run to try to deal with the pain. Holding onto God's love and presence to overcome the pain may be so new but can be modeled and taught and received through prayer, repetition, and support. That is your challenge – to help them get to the place where they constantly react as a disciple as their "default position."

"The Lord brought me out into a spacious place; He rescued me because He delights in me." (Psalm 18:19 NIV)

Prayer for the Speaker and the Talk

Precious Lord, You have a way for us to live that is not of this world. It is counter-cultural, but at the same time meant to be a life of joy, laughter, welcome, and service. I pray for this speaker that every day they are growing closer to you, bolder in their living of a Christian life. I pray that they are ridding their life of anything that stands in the way of this. Help them to teach this idea of being a passionate follower, being disciplined, even when it is hard or unpopular. Help them to teach intimacy with You so that serving You and not the world becomes a thing of love delight, and fulfillment. In Your Name, Amen.

Sample Talk:

Introduction

In baseball they have what is known as a starting pitcher and a closer. The point is that the guy who starts the game is not meant to pitch the whole game. His arm will tire. His accuracy may fade. Another pitcher or pitchers will come in near the end and finish off the game once the first guy has done so many pitches or innings.

Life isn't like that for us though, is it? We are the starter and the closer! Our job is to start and finish our life and hopefully end as well or better than what we did in the beginning and in the middle.

The Apostle Paul said near the end of his life, "I have fought the good fight. I have finished the race, I have kept the faith." (2 Timothy 4:7 NIV)

Hopefully, we will all be able to say this at the end of our lives. "I finished well."

Someone who didn't finish so well was King Solomon. (1 Kings 11:1-13) If you don't know this name, he was a very famous king in ancient Israel. He was the son of another famous man, King David.

Solomon was known for his wisdom and able rule of his people. He became extremely wealthy. He had made God his first priority and many blessings came to him as a result. But...

As his life went on, he got sloppy. He married many women which was permissible in those days, but they were women from other countries and religions. Pretty soon, he was no longer devoting himself to God. He started practicing the faiths of his wives. This led to many bad things. His kingdom was split up after his death. He introduced and allowed dark ideas into his nation and it came unraveled as a result. Solomon's faith was compromised.

He didn't get up every day and say, "I've got to choose to do the next right thing and believe the right beliefs all over again. This is a new day!" He got sloppy about his discipleship – about following God.

Stay Diligent

What is discipleship? Discipleship is putting God first in your life. It is learning all you can about who Jesus is and what He wants us to do and be. It is constantly keeping up practices like worship, prayer, reading your Bible, talking with others about faith. You cannot let these slide or you will start sliding too – backwards!

Jesus would have us forgive others, share with others, protect those weaker than ourselves. There are many concepts in the Christian faith that we need to make regular in our lives. We know we are not to steal or lie or do harm to others. It is important to clean up your language and not cuss if that has been a habit of the past.

Jesus would have us be respectful of authority and honor each other. We are not to seek revenge. There are many practices that make you a Christian and a true follower of Jesus. This is what it means to be a disciple. *It is loving Jesus and doing the things that make you like Him.*

More than one person has told me, if they relapse, before it actually started, they had slacked off on reading the Bible, on prayer, going to church, and so on. There's something to learn from that, isn't there? Stay close to God and He remains close to you and wrong things are kept at arm's length.

Iron Sharpens Iron

What might you do if you feel yourself moving away from discipleship, from following Jesus with your whole heart? In King Solomon's case, he should have cancelled some of those weddings to those foreign women, right?

In your case, what happens if you find yourself drifting away from God? You're not reading your Bible. You're not praying. Rather than forgiving people, you're blowing up at them. That's the time you really need to reach out to God in prayer. "Lord, help me. Why is this happening?" Maybe, that's the time to get certain people or habits out of your life that may be pulling you away from God. But, that's also the time to reach out to people who seem steadier than yourself, isn't it?

If someone else seems full of faith, steady in their discipleship and practice of spiritual activities, why don't you say to them, "Hey, I am having a hard time. Could you read the Bible with me? Could you pray with me? Can I talk with you?"

The Bible says that "as iron sharpens iron, so one person sharpens another." (Proverbs 27:17 NIV) If you get around someone who's really pursuing God, they will hopefully pull you back in their direction and in the direction of God.

I remember one time being in a boat with an older, wiser pastor named Ed. Pastor Ed said, "Do you know why we go to church once a week?" "No," we said, "Why?" He said, "Because that's just about long enough for us to forget everything we heard the week before and to need to hear it all over again."

Gardens Need Care

We forget. We lose our momentum. We get pulled away by other things. Our heart is like a garden. We have got to feed and water it or the good things being planted in it by God will die. We have to keep pulling the "weeds" out or they will quickly choke the things being planted by God.

Yes, it would be nice to accept Jesus in your heart by faith and then say, "Well, that's that. I am all set. I don't have to work on that anymore for the rest of my life." But that's not how discipleship works. To become more like Jesus, to keep doing the next right thing, we've got to study, learn, pray, work at our faith, at the same time, rest in God. That doesn't seem to make sense, does it? Which is it? Do I need to work, or do I need to rest?

The answer is a little of both. We put our eyes on Jesus. We nurture our loving relationship with Him. We give Him our lives. We keep looking to Him, to His beauty, strength, and grace, and we let Him help us. But "looking at Him" involves our opening our Bibles, meditating on the words there, being in worship services, praying, etc. We cannot grow or remain strong in Christian faith without discipline, the discipline of a daily walk with Christ. Your staying close to Him pushes out other influences that might tear you down. Stay close! Practice your faith. The things you've heard about walking with Jesus, put them into practice. Then you will be building your house upon the Solid Rock.

Jesus loves you. Keep Him close.

Questions for the Small Group Session

1. What do you find easiest about the Christian life? What do you find to be the hardest thing?

2. Do you have someone mentoring you, teaching you what being a Christian really means? Are you mentoring someone else? Do you need help in being or becoming a mentor?

3. Unfortunately, some people have thought that being a Christian means going to church and behaving there yet running the rest of the week the way they think is best. What's wrong with this?

4. Is there an area of your life that you have not allowed God to touch? Why is that?

5. What do you think Jesus meant when He talked about "taking up *your* cross and following Me?"

8

From Resentment to Contentment

Key Verse

I am not saying this because I am in need, for I have learned to be content whatever the circumstances. I know what it is to be in need, and I know what it is to have plenty. I have learned the secret of being content in any and every situation, whether well fed or hungry, whether living in plenty or in want. I can do all this through him who gives me strength. (Philippians 4:11-13 NIV)

Issues for the Speaker to Consider

Many of us have heard the expression, "Resentment is like taking poison and hoping someone else will die." It's hard to know who should get the credit for this quote, it has been used so widely. But, probably, the people recovering from addiction with whom you are working have heard it said in AA meetings. It has become popular in Twelve Step settings, so they will get it and chuckle. But laughing at the irony is far removed from learning how to get free of resentful, offended feelings as your "way of life" and regular response to a multitude of situations.

Imagine a young child growing up in an extended family of addicts. Imagine being left alone among people in drug-induced stupors, or having absent parents, the child trying to get food, get sleep, and get to school on their own. Imagine if some of those drug disabled adults are also violent or molesters. This child grows up with fear, strategies to avoid being hurt, and a grand sense of abandonment. This child grows up with some massive soul wounds forming. In other words, they begin to see all the world as a scary place of undependable and rejecting people.

As a child, their responses might be fear and flight. Perhaps as they grow, they harden, get jaded, still see people as undependable as they view the world around them through their wounded thoughts and memories. So, then, as an adult, countless acts and words, even if innocent and not meant with harm, can become the basis for fresh offense and resentment, a seething mass of grudges beneath the surface and a perception of the world that says, "They're all up to no good. They're out to get me. I hate them."

This is only one simulation of how a mindset of being constantly offended could be created. We live in a world where

> We live in a world where many people jump to conclusions and work out scenarios in their thoughts that bear little resemblance to reality.

many people jump to conclusions and work out scenarios in their thoughts that bear little resemblance to reality. They reach the conclusion that someone is doing them wrong or will do them wrong whether or not that is the case. This propensity to be offended, especially based not on current reality, but coming from the haunting of the past, is way too widespread. And among a population of wounded, addicted people who may have missed out on much of their prior life due to their childhood suffering, and then to their own period of addiction, the tendency to be resentful and offended can be "off the charts."

You have much "plowing and planting" to do in this "field," to reap a harvest of changed lives.

It's so important to teach through stories and repetition that many times we react with offense when the other person is innocent, or at least, clumsy in their communication or behavior, and our offense is not based on them, but is coming out of an area in us that needs repair.

How many times do people get divorced, break up friendships, quit jobs, leave churches, split churches, and so on because they have not gotten over the broken places in themselves? Some people keep repeating and repeating the same scenarios – for example, they join a church, are enthused about the church, someone seems to "snub" them, and then they are out of the church. Then they join another church, they're enthused about the church, someone seems to "snub" them, and they are out of the church. The offended behavior repeats and repeats until it is identified, healed, and stopped. And you can substitute, "they make a friend until…," or "they get married until…" If people are not taught the nature of getting repeatedly offended often over nothing, if they don't see the wounds in their own souls, they are destined to be offended often perpetually.

And offense can make us physically sick.

Many Christian healers who have a lengthy history of physical healing will tell you that they often have to get at the emotional root of the person's problems and then the physical problem gets healed and more importantly, remains healed, because broken emotions are not around to cause it to return.

The late John Wimber of the Vineyard Church told a story of a woman who had "chronic stomach disorders and arthritis" and they did not get better with prayer. But, in interviewing her, it was discovered that she had an estranged relationship with her sister. Her sister had married a man that this woman loved, and then later divorced him. Wimber had had the impression of bitterness as he prayed for her. (This story will be in the sample talk.)

She was encouraged to forgive her sister (not based upon any change in her sister, but out of obedience to God's instruction to "forgive one another as you have been forgiven in Christ.") She wrote the letter but delayed taking action for a while. When she did finally go to the mailbox, as soon as she dropped the letter in the slot, she felt better. By the time she got home, she was totally healed.[19]

Offense and physical illness, in addition to mental pain, i.e. "eating the poison," all can go together. Forgiveness, learning to see people in a benevolent way, looking past their foibles, gives us a peace and refreshment, a light-weightedness in God that is delightful.

So, what precisely do you need to teach your recovery audience in this session?

1. Current bitterness is often based on old experiences.

2. Wounds get formed in our soul which is the place of our emotions, thinking, and decision making.

3. We then react to other people, not so much on the basis of their current words or behavior, but more out of our brokenness.

4. Our memories and perception of the world can be healed through Jesus Christ, the cross, His resurrection, and the power of the Holy Spirit in us.

5. Sometimes, people truly are offensive, rude, thoughtless, selfish, etc., but as Christians we can learn to not just imitate Jesus but have His resurrected life work through us towards them.

6. We can learn to say, "I forgive them. They don't know what they are doing" again and again and again. And pray for them.

7. We can stay at peace like Jesus, not making our comfort level or contentment be based on people's treatment of us, good or bad, because He is in us and with us.

8. We can make our state of mind and contentment be based on the constant goodness of God and His love for us.

9. No matter how angry we have been, we can learn to live without it.

I have talked with many people in recovery, as one of their pastors, and heard hair-raising stories of abuse at the hands of family members, even attempts on their lives. I have heard of sexual abuse at the hands of family members and others, stories of gang rapes, things that are so deeply disturbing. But I have also urged these same people to forgive the perpetrators while still seeing the behavior as reprehensible.

I remember one person who told me of sexual abuse at the hands of a family member and of their desire to kill that family

JESUS AND THE ADDICT

member. They even described efforts to try to kill the family member.

We discussed the nature of the abuse. We talked about this person's hatred and attempted murder of their family member. I asked the person if they were ready to forgive their family member right at that moment because they had said to me, "Someday, *maybe* I'll try and forgive my family member."

I said, "How about now? Could you trust me and more especially, God, to take this step now?"

There was agreement and we began the prayer, asking God for the power and the willingness to forgive the family member though the behavior had been heinous. I then encouraged the person with me to repent and ask for God's forgiveness for hatred and violence and that God would grant freedom from these feelings and behaviors forever. By the end of this prayer, tears were flowing, and it became a moment where a prayer for salvation in Jesus Christ was willingly prayed.

> But Christian scripture does not coach us to be people of perpetual unforgiveness and self-pity.

The word resentment can be defined as having "bitter indignation at being unfairly treated."[20] Often people who are angry and resentful may find naïve sympathy from others. "Oh, you poor thing. Of course, you feel badly. You have every right to feel this and to remain in these feelings. You are a victim."

149

But Christian scripture does not coach us to be people of perpetual unforgiveness and self-pity. We are advised to do the opposite of what comes naturally "in the flesh." I love the King James version of wonderful verses from Luke 6 about how we are to live as Christian people. The language is very effective. Here is just one of them:

"Bless them who curse you and pray for those who spitefully use you." (Luke 6:28 NKJV)

Jesus did not call down curses from the cross, as we know from the details of the crucifixion in the Bible. Rather, among His seven last words were these:

"'Father forgive them, for they do not know what they are doing.' And they divided up his clothes by casting lots." (Luke 23:34 NIV)

Even to the very end, most everyone around Jesus was being "offensive," and that is putting it mildly, but His posture was to forgive and not take it into Himself. Belief in and life with Jesus has the potential to make all of us, including those in recovery, people who can be *unoffendable* like Jesus. When we are that way, there will be no more poison that we're ingesting hoping others will die. We will be free. Help your recovery learners to understand this big idea of Christianity. We must forgive seventy times seven, that is, all the time. (Matthew 18:22)

Prayer for the Speaker and the Talk

Precious Lord, help this speaker to examine his or her own life and see what tendency they have to feel offended. Help him or her to then listen to you, Holy Spirit. Are there old wounds out of which the world is being seen now?

Bring healing to this speaker. And then, in turn, help them to show the precious people they are guiding how to walk out of old wounds, see the world through today's eyes, and walk in the forgiveness of Jesus as their new lifestyle. Let it be said of them, that they are in Christ and therefore, a new creation. The old is gone. The new has come. In Jesus' name, Amen

Sample Talk:

Introduction

My father was in the Navy. We didn't hear too many war stories, but I remember one. He told us the story of two men who worked in the officers' dining room on the ship on which he was serving. He said one night they got into a knife fight over whether to leave the lights on or off in this room.

As I said, it was war time, and lights were to be kept off at certain times to avoid bombing, but I think the foolishness of this fight was that the lighting of this room could not be seen outside of the ship. They were trying to kill each other over a non-problem.

But why? Was it really about the lights or about something else?

Sometimes, we can get so offended at someone in front of us, but our feelings really aren't about them or even the current situation. It has to do with other things going on within us.

Maybe the two men in the officers' "mess" had been pushed around or frightened enough times in previous situations that this moment was the tipping point and all the pent-up feelings from other times just blew up towards each other. Having a deadly knife fight over lights that didn't matter seems a little much, doesn't it?

We have got to learn not to take the bait of satan. His bait is for us to get offended, forget about God's ways, and do whatever we can to have our way which may include severely or subtly hurting someone else. This is bad for us and for others! Not only can we hurt people, but there can be a connection between illness and resentment.

A pastor named John Wimber told the story of a woman who was bitter at her sister for a betrayal over a man that had happened years before. This woman, when Wimber prayed for her, had arthritis and chronic stomach pain.

He advised her to write her sister and to forgive her, a piece of advice that the woman took some time to follow. But the day she took her letter reaching out to her sister and dropped it in the mailbox was the day of her starting to feel better. She felt relief when she dropped the letter in the mailbox and total healing by the time she drove home. Physical illness, mental pain, all these things can be attached to an attitude of offense.

The Apostle Paul said that it doesn't have to be this way. We can learn the secret of contentment, so that we don't fly off the handle or even lose a day to grumbling. He wrote about contentment in this way:

> …I have learned to be content whatever the circumstances. I know what it is to be in need, and I know what it is to have plenty. I have learned the secret of being content in any and every situation, whether well fed or hungry, whether living in plenty or in want. I can do all this through him who gives me strength." (Philippians 4:11-13 NIV)

Now, Paul didn't write that because he had an easy life with no struggle and no opponents. No! His life was extremely hard. Here is a description of how much he had been through:

> …I have worked much harder, been in prison more frequently, been flogged more severely, and been exposed to death again and again. Five times I received from the Jews the forty lashes minus one. Three times I was beaten with rods, once I was pelted with stones, three times I was shipwrecked, I spent a night and a day in the open sea, I have been constantly on the move. I have been in danger from rivers, in danger from bandits,

in danger from my fellow Jews, in danger from Gentiles; in danger in the city in danger in the country, in danger at sea; and in danger from false believers. I have labored and toiled and have often gone without sleep; I have known hunger and thirst and have often gone without food; I have been cold and naked. (2 Corinthians 11:23-27 NIV)

If anyone had a right to be in a bad mood and feel righteously grumpy, it was Paul. But no, he did not let himself feel moody, angry, or sad and feel justified in that. Rather, he had learned to stay in a place of evenness, concern for others, and contentment.

How did he do this? Let's break down his words on contentment and find the answer for our own lives.

Contentment Takes Learning

Paul wrote that he had *learned* to be content. When he used the word "learned," he not only meant that he had gained more ideas and teaching about what contentment is and how to have it through God. He also meant that by using that knowledge and *practicing* it, he was becoming much better at remaining content all the time.

What he was saying is that you learn that such a thing is possible. Here, Paul said it. "I have learned the secret of being content in every situation." Wow! He had practiced this enough that he could maintain this state of mind at all times. That meant he had to have repeated situations where learning could occur. In that sense, it was good that he struggled. In it, he learned.

And, we know, when you are practicing and trying to learn something, sometimes you do great and sometimes you mess up. Paul is telling us we're going to have moments when we aren't content, when we will still get resentful.

We are learners! When we see that happening, what should we do? Judge ourselves and give up? No! The answer at that moment is to go to God and say, "Father, I am irritated and offended again (and I just got up! Ha!) Please forgive me. Help me to start over. I repent of irritation and offended thoughts. I repent of my grumpiness. Help me now to forgive, to be filled with grace and gratitude and to release all bitterness. In Jesus' name. Amen."

With that, you try again. You remind yourself that being offended, resentful, and bitter primarily hurts you although it may upset people around you too. That's another reason to work on your attitude. You want to be someone who lifts people up, not one who brings them down. And you want to bring people to faith, not away from it. If you are going to be a sourpuss, stop wearing your gold cross – that's bad PR for Jesus, right?

Contentment Can be in Every Situation

There is a story in Acts 16 beginning at verse sixteen about Paul and Silas being wrongly imprisoned while on a missionary trip. Not only that, they were severely beaten and put in stocks holding their feet. At midnight, these two Christian leaders were singing praise songs and praying. Suddenly, there was an earthquake, the prison doors flew open and everyone's chains came loose. As a result, the jailer and his whole family became Christians and Paul and Silas went free. It's an amazing story of a miracle of God's power.

But, I am telling you this because of the first part of the story. They were singing and praying in prison *after* being beaten and unfairly locked up. They were content and trusting God that everything would work out. And it did!

In the verses we're looking at from Philippians, Paul wrote, "I know what it is to be in need, and I know what it is to have plenty. I have learned the secret of being content in any and every situation, whether well fed or hungry, whether living in plenty or want."

Paul was saying he had figured out how to stay on an "even keel" whether in extremely good times or in extremely bad times or just on ordinary days. He had tapped into a secret of God and now things didn't throw him all over the place the way they do to so many of us. Some of us live on an emotional roller coaster, but the truth is, that with God, it doesn't have to be this way.

Contentment Comes from Jesus

Just a few verses before this, Paul wrote in Philippians 4:4-7 that we ought to

Rejoice in the Lord always. I will say it again: Rejoice! Let your gentleness be evident to all. The Lord is near. Do not be anxious about anything, but in every situation, by prayer and petition, with thanksgiving, present your requests to God. And the peace of God, which transcends all understanding, will guard your hearts and your minds in Christ Jesus. (NIV)

There it is, the secret. → V13 I can do all things through Him who strengthens me.

The way to be in supernatural peace, unoffendable, in the peace of God, is to dwell on Jesus Christ. Paul says, "rejoice in Him always." That probably sounds impossible when things are tough, but it is the greatest secret weapon you can have as a Christian. When it seems totally unnatural to praise and sing and pray to the Lord, do it. It may take every ounce of strength to speak a Bible verse over yourself but do it. Those words are living and active and full of power. (Hebrews 4:12) The atmosphere changes, you change, nothing can get at you as you retreat into the Lord and rest in Him.

The secret of contentment is to keep your attention fixed on Jesus and His love for you. The secret is to think of His strength, not your weakness, and certainly to not dwell on your difficulties or the difficult people around you.

Keep your eyes on Jesus. Fix them upon Him. He will give you strength to remain calm, to bear with certain things, to get to the other side of your trouble. He will help you to remain calm in the face of enemies and to pray for them. He will fight the battle for you.

This passage says, "I can do all things through Him who gives me strength."

Contentment Reveals My Level of Trust

A final thought for you. If you're easily irritated or outright angry a lot of the time, what does it say about your relationship with God? Does that state of mind say that maybe you are not really close to God yet? Maybe you don't really trust Him?

Yes, it does say that.

But, don't be hard on yourself. Just recognize the problem and your own need. Say to yourself, "I don't really think God is working on my behalf or that He'll come through for me – not yet. That's why I get frustrated and angry so easily sometimes even at really little things."

And then pray, "Lord, help me. Be more real for me than You ever have been before. Let me encounter You in new ways. Touch my heart. Speak to me in ways that I can hear. Help me to stop being afraid. Help me to believe that You've got a special path marked out for me and You will guide me on it. I don't want to be a grouch. I don't want to be sick because I am resentful. Heal me, Lord, and I will be healed."

You can do this. God's got you. He hasn't brought you this far to drop you. He'll help you to get peaceful, trusting, and content, just like Paul.

Questions for the Small Group Session

1. If there was such a thing as a "bitter-ometer," a machine that could measure bitterness, where would the needle be on your level of bitterness towards people, low, medium, high, or on emergency alert, machine about to blow up?

2. Seriously, how easily do you get offended at people?

3. Did the talk make sense to you, that some of your resentment has nothing to do with the person in front of you, but is based on past experiences?

4. How can you heal those past experiences, according to what you heard tonight?

5. Does it make sense to you that resentment can make you physically sick?

6. Do you have anything going on in your body right now that might get better if you forgave somebody? Are you ready?

.

9

Stomping on Fear

Key Verses

"I sought the LORD, and he answered me; he delivered me from all my fears." (Psalm 34:4 NIV)

Can anything ever separate us from Christ's love? Does it mean he no longer loves us if we have trouble or calamity, or are persecuted, or hungry, or destitute, or in danger, or threatened with death?...No, despite all these things, overwhelming victory is ours through Christ, who loved us. And I am convinced that nothing can ever separate us from God's love. Neither death nor life, neither angels nor demons, neither our fears for today nor our worries about tomorrow – not even the powers of hell can separate us from God's love. No power in the sky above or in the earth below – indeed, nothing in all creation will ever be able to separate us from the love of God that is revealed in Christ Jesus our Lord." (Romans 8:35, 37-39 NLT)

Issues for the Speaker to Consider

I remember sitting in a Bible study in a church in which I was leading as pastor. We were studying the passage shown above from Romans 8. Our reader for the morning was a young woman who was a recovering addict. She was reading from The Life Recovery Bible in the New Living Translation. This Bible, as you may know, is specifically designed for people in recovery and weaves in the Twelve Steps of Alcoholics Anonymous to help make AA's recovery principles connect with the message of the Bible stories.

What struck me that morning was the New Living Translation's wonderful way of presenting v. 35, "Does it mean [Christ] no longer loves us if we have trouble or calamity, or are persecuted, or hungry, or destitute, or in danger or threatened with death? NO!!!"

This young woman had experienced trouble, calamity, sleeping in abandoned houses with nothing to eat, prostitution, having not a dime to her name, being threatened with guns and violence and people out to get her. She had been used by men and had used them back. Her children were from multiple fathers, the most recent father still around, but the relationship rocky. She had seen hell on earth, some of it her own making. I had witnessed the cold calculation of several of her relatives any time she had a little more money and safety in her life; how they would move in and try to remove any largesse of which they became aware. She did not quite yet understand the love of the One she was reading about, but she had certainly known her fair share of fear. That she knew well. And this verse, reassuring her and the others listening, that the one thing she would always be able to count on could be Jesus, was so stirring, spoken in her voice. Jesus would never abandon her if she would truly choose Him. Nor were her troubles a sign of Him moving away or holding displeasure towards her. Her troubles were the result of attacks upon her by people, or were the outcome of her own poor choices, but Jesus could be and always would be the source of security and hope, even in a chaotic set of circumstances. That was what she was reading over herself that morning. And it was reassuring for all of us. His peace filled the room.

One emotion that is strongly present in recovery communities, though it may be well-masked in public, is fear.

What fears are present? Below is a short list. You, as a sponsor, a speaker, a teacher, or a pastor with those in recovery, are probably well-acquainted with these, and undoubtably can add more or list fears unique to your setting.

Think about these fears as you prepare to talk to your community. God would deliver the people from all of them:

1. Relapse. Relapse. Relapse.

2. Loss of child custody.

3. Relationship with children not being redeemable.

4. Pregnancy, afraid of what's coming next.

5. Permanent poverty. Being unable to pay bills.

6. Riding the bus.

7. Being near old "playgrounds and playmates." (former drug connections)

8. Losing face.

9. People's opinions.

10. Being bullied.

11. Being a bully. Afraid of one's own violence.

12. Not being able to measure up.

13. Getting a job.

14. Not getting a job.

15. Starting classes.

16. Finishing classes.

17. Fear of old abusers finding out new location.

18. Being unloved/alone.

19. Sexual desires unmet or out of control.

20. Racing thoughts.

21. Panic/anxiety attacks, other mental health issues.

22. Speaking in front of a group.

23. Crowds.

24. Health Issues.

25. Not being able to get help for health issues and afford it.

26. Not being able to sleep.

27. Family problems/estrangements.

28. Court/legal issues. Completing probation, parole. Staying out of trouble.

29. Old warrants becoming active.

30. Being left behind.

These fears may be masked behind bluster, or silence. Hopefully, there is a roommate, counselor, or small group setting where they can be shared and start to be addressed. But it is so important to speak about fear and help people understand that it is usually the first emotion that is experienced when negative feelings arise. In other words, if there is an angry meltdown that a recovering addict experiences with a leader, a roommate or someone else, more than likely, the first thing going on was fear about something happening in their life.

As is listed above, not wanting to lose face is a very real concern for many in the community so helping your listeners to be open about this topic rather than sitting stone-faced without response will be your task. Humor is so helpful to break the ice and let truth and transparency enter a room. When a person has felt beaten down by many seemingly more powerful than them, be it an abuser, or the legal system, the coping mechanism can be to hide feelings and needs. Continually teaching that Jesus is about grace and new life becomes so important. People need to see that they don't have to be afraid about being real about their feelings, particularly fear, because the aim of God is always to heal and lift us up.

A verse that I feel particularly blesses the recovery community is Isaiah 54:4:

> Do not be afraid; you will not be put to shame. Do not fear disgrace; you will not be humiliated. You will forget the shame of your youth and remember no more the reproach of your widowhood. (NIV)

The goal of God is to lift heads and let people walk out of their pasts through His salvation in Christ. He is not about shame and guilt and embarrassment.

A moving story that demonstrates this comes from Luke 19:1-10, the story of Zacchaeus, the chief tax collector. Hated by the townspeople and guilty of cheating fellow citizens, Jesus calls him down from the tree where he has been watching Jesus pass by.

Jesus tells him He must stay at his house that day. Touched by Jesus' acceptance, he gives up his crooked ways and promises to make amends. The way of Jesus is to free people from what they have been and return

> **The goal of God is to lift heads and let people walk out of their pasts through His salvation in Christ.**

them supernaturally to being sons and daughters of God without shame or fear.

And so, one more beautiful verse on fear:

"There is no fear in love; but perfect love casts out fear: because fear involves torment. But he who fears has not been made perfect in love." (1 John 4:18 NKJV)

Fear is a terribly tormenting emotion, keeping us bound and locked up in a stuck place where we cannot go forward. Fear keeps a person from being all God intended them to be. It takes hold of the mind and blocks out healthy thoughts and decision making.

The Bible even mentions a "spirit of fear," such that we know there is a demonic element of cornering a person so as to stifle their growth and their connection to God.

What will be some of the antidotes to being consumed with fear and being paralyzed?

You will need to teach how scripture can be used – memorized, prayed, and declared over a person such that their thoughts are moved from the negative to the positive.

You will have to explain and promote the power of worship and praise – how it causes one to rise from a cowering, defeated position to a bold and victorious one.

Your listeners will have to learn how to walk out of a fear one step at a time. They may need help to outline a plan for overcoming all-consuming fears.

Teach and demonstrate the power of persistent prayer for transforming what goes on in our minds.

In talking about and recognizing that there may be a spiritual component, a spirit of fear at work, you will again need to stress the idea of assertive spiritual warfare.

And as has been mentioned, humor and self-deprecating stories about overcoming one's own fears, will be enormously helpful.

People can become bold where they once felt beaten down. We can come to sincerely hold the conviction that

> The Lord will grant that the enemies who rise up against you will be defeated before you. They will come at you from one direction but flee from you in seven. (Deuteronomy 28:7 NIV)

And that as we stand firm and believe God, our "mountains will jump into the sea." (Mark 11:23)

But wherever your listeners are in their battle against fear, they can trust the heart of God to be for them. He is not condemning of us as we try to overcome worry. Again, returning to the Romans 8 passage that opened this section, we can be comforted that "neither our fears for today or our worries about tomorrow" can separate us from the love of God in Christ Jesus. Even as we try to grow up and out of fear with the help of God, He still loves us. He is still with us. He is for us.

Prayer for the Speaker and the Talk

Lord, if we could face down fear and eliminate it from our lives, many of our other negative emotions and actions from resentment, rage, and unbelief to gossip, grumbling, and lethargy would disappear. Help us, O Lord. Help us to so trust You that the words, "The Lord is my light and salvation, whom shall I fear?" become absolutely the foundation of who we are. Help this speaker to transmit boldness, bravery, joy, and yet humble trust and dependence upon You. Help the speaker to model a way of life and belief that You are always with us and You are always fighting our battles. Let the listeners become braver and more believing because of what is said and the way it is said in this talk. In Jesus' name, Amen

Sample Talk:

Introduction

When I was a child I was one major chicken.

Everything seemed to scare me. As a 9-year-old at the swimming pool, taking lessons, I was asked to jump off the LOW diving board. Long after the class cleared out and the pool area was entirely empty, there sat my mother on the bleachers while I stood at the end of the board frozen in fear.

While at a relatives' farm, I remember hiding in the bathroom because us city kids had been invited to ride on the family's pony. Note I said pony, not horse. This was a small animal. Maybe because she was named Ginger, I was afraid she would be a little spicy, but she wasn't. I was just afraid – *again*!

I can remember at twelve coming home in tears from school because the teacher had said if we wrote a sentence that was too long we would get an F. I had a good grade in English, there was no way I was going to get an F. But I was so afraid, I had worked myself into hysterics.

Some of you may think this sounds like crazy talk – maybe you've braved some pretty hair-raising situations with real fear-producing danger, and I'm talking about writing a long sentence in middle school but bear with me. I am trying to point out how gripping fear can be and sometimes it's based on things that are not going to happen. And sometimes, it can be about the smallest of things. I was not going to get hurt on the diving board or the horse or get a bad grade. But, I was like that as a little girl - also shy – often afraid of my own shadow. Maybe somewhere I had gotten the idea that I needed to be perfect and do all these things without a flaw. So, I was afraid to try.

Well, my fears lasted until college. I used to be so scared to have to get up in front of a class and speak. A lot of people will say that's their biggest fear, too, to talk in front of people. When I had that assignment, my hands and my voice would shake.

But the day came when all this began to change, and it began to change because of God and because I decided to fight this enemy called fear.

At the same time that I was still struggling with speaking in college, I fell in love with horses and began to go riding and got so I loved when I put my horse into a run. I remember an evening ride with some friends on a beach in Mexico. So exhilarating! Just by taking classes to learn to ride and getting on horses again and again, and learning to groom and saddle them, I got over the fear. Fear went away as I step by step faced the thing of which I was afraid and learned how to handle it.

Swimming and diving boards – the same thing. I just faced the fear and learned to do the thing step by step. I even tried surfing when I was a teenager and lived near the ocean.

But the thing of speaking before crowds – that was <u>all</u> God. Where I had been intensely shy and terrified of getting up before crowds, as God called me to professional ministry, He gave me the gift not only to preach before a crowd, but He gave me the capacity to enjoy it. I often tell people that when I preach I feel like a sight we so often see in the Midwest – like a hawk soaring on the wind, circling over the plains. I feel unstoppable and full of joy. And I have had the chance to preach before thousands, even act in church plays.

God has the same plan and desire for each one here that no matter what you are afraid of, no matter how many fears you have, He would set you free from all of them so that you can soar and fully be the person that He always meant for you to be. No matter how big those fears are!

The Bible declares this to be true – that it is God's heart to free you:

"I sought the LORD, and he answered me; he delivered me from all my fears." (Psalm 34:4 NIV)

How beautiful these words are and how hopeful! Let's study this verse together tonight and see a process by which you can get free from fear and live your life wholly and happily.

What does the verse tell us first?

Seek God

We get a blueprint for how to get rid of fear in this simple verse. The first words "I sought the LORD," mean that the answer is in and with God. Yes, we can take baby steps to get over some fears, breaking down the thing we're trying to conquer into manageable steps. If you are afraid to ride the bus to your job or treatment, for example, you can get the bus schedule and go over it with friends. You can walk to the place where you are to catch the bus and prepare yourself for that. You can ask a friend who is familiar with taking the bus to go with you a few times.

These are simple steps you can take to make your fear of something more manageable.

But honestly, the best place for any of us to start is always with God because our goal is to get over fear, in general. Period. We want to be fearless people who can manage the things we have to do now as well as take on new challenges.

So, what does it mean to "seek the LORD." In the original language back in ancient days, the word for "sought" meant a few different things. Yes, it meant to look for, to try to understand, to go after, to follow, but it also meant "to worship."[21]

So, to seek the LORD means to really go after His heart for you and His help for you. And where do you do that? Well, reading the Bible and finding verses about His help and specifically His help with fear would give you insight into how much He wants to take the fear away. More importantly, the word of God has actual supernatural power to change your life as you declare it over yourself and believe it.

When you worship at church or in a small group or by yourself, chances are as you sing songs you love or as you pray, you will feel good feelings rise up in your heart as well as strength and hope that you can overcome difficulties. Your outlook will begin to change in God's presence.

One time my husband was home dealing with chemo for his cancer and I was several states away from him, preparing to give a talk at a conference. I called him just before the evening session of the conference and he said he was sick and miserable, laying on the couch. He felt like he had a terrible case of the flu. This was the effect of his treatment.

I went into the session and began to feel sad. Sad because I was not home to help him. But why else? Because I was afraid. Fear is often the first thing you feel, and then other emotions come in on top of it. I was afraid for my husband's health. Afraid of losing him as we had been several years in this battle. Afraid I couldn't cover my emotions in the crowd around me.

The pastor leading that night was serving communion and singing some of the lines of the communion service. My husband and I had gotten into the habit of having communion daily, feeling it to be a healing meal. So, that added to my tenderness emotionally, particularly hearing the words sung. We were having communion and my husband was not there. I wanted to leave and go back to my room and cry.

After receiving communion, though, I went to the altar to kneel and pray. I began to ask God to take care of my husband and to take away his pain and suffering. As I knelt, I felt as if the

Holy Spirit had knelt beside me and had put His arm around me. It was an incredible moment. I felt Him begin to whisper gently, "Don't leave. Stay here. Worship. Trust Me."

Whether I realized it or not, I had been seeking the LORD and He answered me.

God Answers

That's the second part of the Psalm verse, isn't it? I sought the LORD and He answered me. By the way, the word LORD, with the letters all in capitals is often explained in Bible introductions as being the way of saying one of the names of God. You may or may not have heard this before, but the name is Yahweh or Jehovah. What is important about this form of God's name is to know one of its ideas is of God being close and intimate, living among us.

I felt the Holy Spirit kneeling by me, comforting me, encouraging me to fight off the fear, sadness, and heaviness in His strength, not my own. As I said, it was as if His arm was around me, His voice in my ear. "Stay!" I went back to my seat and began to sing. I was still wiping away tears, and in a tiny little voice, hardly audible, I began to join in with the people around me. Thank goodness it was dark in the auditorium! I was still pretty blubbery!

"O, the blood of Jesus," I half-whispered at first. It was an aching effort to get the words out. But bit by bit, I began to grow in strength. Soon, I was singing rather loudly and swaying like a gospel choir member. "O, the blood of Jesus." What a great song choice!

God Takes Fear Away

As I said, I was not doing this in my own strength. The Holy Spirit was flowing in with His manifest presence and power, giving me more and more strength. The Holy Spirit is in us, but He also can come upon us more to help us in our time of need. He lifted me up and delivered me right out of the very challenging feelings I was having. I soon felt joy and a desire to help others. I was part of the altar ministry team that night and I had almost left to go be miserable in my hotel room, and not pray for anyone. What a temptation that was from the enemy! If he could have gotten me in this, he could get me again and again. But the Holy Spirit intervened and lifted me up and out of fear and sorrow. He took my eyes off myself and my troubles. I "prayed up a storm" that night, loving the chance to help others. I felt strong!

He Will Take All Fear

It is God's heart for us to be aware of His powerful presence always and to be set free from all fear not just some. He wants to help us approach life from the position of a saved, beloved, and victorious member of His family. This is the message of this Psalm verse. "He delivered me from *all* my fears."

And this has been my own experience with God. He has again and again taken away fears and replaced them with holy boldness and a sense of my position in Him. It is in this four step process, seeking Him, looking for Him to answer, watching for His deliverance, and believing that He desires and is able to take away all, not just some, of your fears, that you will be freed.

There is a little more to tell you about the story above. A few weeks later, I told my husband what had happened at the meeting. I was emotional again, telling him how I had been lifted up by the Spirit to keep going and rejoice even though the circumstances were hard and remained hard. My husband almost seemed to not be listening. He was staring into space. Suddenly he looked directly at me and said, "What time did you start this worshipping and fighting off of fear?" I said, "Around seven to eight maybe, Georgia time."

He said, "Wow! It was about that time that I suddenly began to feel much better. I got up off the couch, ate a little food, and walked the dog." We were then even more moved. Not only had the Lord lifted my spirits and removed my heaviness and fear, but healing and relief had flowed into my husband while I worshipped in the Spirit in Georgia.

Praise and worship powerfully push back our enemies. Especially fear. Praise be to the God who delivers us out of all our fears and brings us peace.

Questions for the Small Group Session

1. If you feel like sharing, what is your biggest fear?

2. How do you cope with fear?

3. Does it make sense that sometimes when you're mad or stirred up in some way, that really, underneath all that, you are first feeling fear?

4. When you are afraid, do you pray? Do you worship? How do you feel afterwards?

5. Have you learned a scripture yet that helps you to feel less afraid when you say it and pray it? What is it? It might help the rest of the group.

10
Learning Patience

Key Verses

And that's not all. We are full of joy even when we suffer. We know that our suffering gives us the strength to go on. The strength to go on produces character. Character produces hope. And hope will never bring us to shame. That's because God's love has been poured into our hearts. This happened through the Holy Spirit, who has been given to us. (Romans 5:3-5 NIrV)

"But let patience have its perfect work, that you may be perfect and complete, lacking nothing." (James 1:4 NKJV)

Issues for the Speaker to Consider

One of the states of mind I have observed with many people with whom I have done pastoral counseling in recovery is impatience.

Someone will talk to me who has only recently entered the recovery community and they will say something like this, "I have got to get out of here and get a job. I have got to get some money. I can't be on probation for a month without my phone (the rule of the community). I've got to get my kids back. I've got to have rent money, get an apartment. I have got to get going. I have no time for all of this waiting." They are agitated and focused on logistics only.

Disney World, as you may know, has a system called "fast pass," where you can sign up for a ride in advance and at the appointed time zip on in ahead of everyone else who has been waiting in the regular line for a long time. Many of these impatient folks in recovery are looking for their fast pass to a new life.

Another way this impatience presents itself is that they may try to be the "top of the class" in the recovery community. They have already mastered everything they need to learn in treatment or in the various small group gatherings, be they recovery oriented or spiritual. "I've got this," they may say. "I've got it better than everyone around me. I am ready to move on."

The challenge is to help them see that they have been in addiction for a long time (in many cases). They are well-formed in that lifestyle and in the thinking that goes along with it. They've got lots of wounds. Making sure that they are truly well and can reliably live in a different fashion is going to take some time. Being sure that sobriety and responsibility become the real foundation of their new life is a process. Helping them to grow in new found faith – discipling them – will take time. They owe it to themselves and all those who love them to be very patient and to take the time to truly be healed. Dry drunks fall down again way too easily. Real through and through healing is needed. "Let patience have its perfect work," as stated in James 1:4 above is the needed mindset. Beneath the rush to get to the next step is anxiety about being able to accomplish goals and fear that they will be left behind.

Patience is one of the fruits of the Spirit and explanation about its spiritual nature is needed:

"But the Holy Spirit produces this kind of fruit in our lives: love, joy, peace, patience, kindness, goodness, faithfulness, gentleness, and self-control..." (Galatians 5:22-23 NLT)

In other words, patience is something that will grow out of a relationship with God through Jesus Christ, empowered by the Holy Spirit. Patience is something God

> **They owe it to themselves and all those who love them to be very patient and to take the time to truly be healed.**

puts in us and grows in our hearts by His presence in us and by His work in us from the inside out.

But what is patience exactly? You are going to have to help your listeners to really grasp the many dimensions of this "virtue."

Patience is when you endure the passage of time as you wait for something to happen. You don't complain. You don't try to force an outcome or hurry things along. You don't try to "jump the gun." You wait with a *good attitude*. That is a form of patience.

> **We need to learn to have patience with ourselves, our families, our healing, our circumstances, and other people.**

Patience is when you have a difficult person or persons with whom you have to interact. Rather than blowing up at them in irritation, you are kind and you look past their annoying words or habits. You don't come down hard on them and you don't push them away. That is patience too.

Patience is when you or a loved one has an illness or difficult situation to endure. Rather than complaining, being full of self-pity, or doing something foolish to try and eradicate the situation, you bear with it, believing relief will come from God. You keep your attitude cheerful.

These are all examples of situations where patience is required. Patience is waiting something out without complaining or doing something foolish to try to get yourself swiftly out of the situation. It is learning to bear with challenging people with kindness and understanding. It is putting up with the passage of time when nothing seems to change. It is all these things.[22]

We need to learn to have patience with ourselves, our families, our healing, our circumstances, and other people. Patience needs to be coupled with a real hope and belief in God's goodness, that He does have a plan for our lives, and that He is working behind the scenes even when we can't see it. Growing into that constant, faith-filled trust in God no matter what is happening takes time.

Getting a firm mindset like that of the prophet Habakkuk in the Old Testament is the goal towards which we try to move in our life of faith. He was able to say:

> Though the fig tree does not bud and there are no grapes on the vines, though the olive crop fails, and the fields produce no food, though there are no sheep in the pen and no cattle in the stalls, yet I will rejoice in the Lord, I will be joyful in God my Savior.

> The Sovereign Lord is my strength; he makes my feet like the feet of a deer, he enables me to tread on the heights. (Habakkuk 3:17-19 NIV)

This is what true patience brings about – a profound trust in God that causes an individual to find joy in God even as circumstances may be hard *and* unchanging! And since patience is a fruit of the Spirit, it is God in us that forms and grows this character trait. Through His strength at work in us, we become able to wait. Out of this patience during suffering comes the possibility to be joyful even in hard times. A person develops a wonderful character that is noble and longsuffering in this way. The person who really has patience and trusts God will believe that God is working and has perfect timing and results that He has designed for us. The promises of God are for us, we can decide when practicing patience. We become willing to wait, even happy in the waiting. The capacity to be patient brings peace of mind.

True patience will enable the person in recovery to take the time needed to get well and to gain the spiritual tools to stay well. True patience will enable the person in recovery not to settle for lesser goals like just finding the next boyfriend or girlfriend or getting an apartment, etc., rather than seeking deep relationship with God and deep personal and lasting healing first.

Jesus said to us that God knows about our daily needs for clothes, food, and rent money so we should "seek first his kingdom and his righteousness, and all these things will be given to you as well." (Matthew 6:33 NIV) This is a hard thing to preach – trust during lack – but it is important to declare it. It is possible to live this way. It is possible to have this great a faith.

True patience will enable the person in recovery to bear with the roommate with the quirky habits or the one who talks too much or whatever the irritating habits may be. Patience from God enables us to not be offended or break off relating to other people. Instead, we learn to see the good in them and to pay attention only to that.

Patience keeps the recovering addict from "running" at the first sign of discomfort. It keeps all of us from road rage and arguments, quitting jobs too easily, and breaking up relationships over nothing. When you are patient, you avoid making big mistakes in decision making and in emotional reactions. Those in recovery will so benefit from being taught exactly what patience is and how to gain it.

There are times when we do need to step out and take action. Learning when and how to do that is also important and there is a balance between waiting and taking faith-filled steps forward in our lives. But often, we need to endure and wait even when things are uncomfortable. And we will be rewarded by the waiting and the godly attitude we possess during the waiting.

Galatians 6:9 says that that we should "not become tired of doing good. At the right time we will gather a crop if we don't give up." (NIrV)

There is so much value in learning to wait and trust, particularly when you are uncomfortable, and the going is tough. This is patience and it is so needed in recovery.

Prayer for the Speaker and the Talk

Heavenly Father, we saw Christ endure the cross for the joy set before Him. He was patient with such severe suffering because He knew the result ahead of Him that would affect the whole world forever. He was patient in other ways, patient with disciples who made all kinds of mistakes and had all kinds of wrong ideas.

Help this speaker, Lord, to be patient with himself or herself, to be patient with the people who are part of the recovery community to whom they are ministering, and to be patient with challenging situations. Help the speaker to, in turn, teach and model this "longsuffering" patience, a way of not getting irritated or complaining, but rather enduring challenges while trusting God.

May this lesson be crystal clear to those listening who desperately need patience for their healing. Amen

Sample Talk:

Introduction

In World War II, a woman named Corrie ten Boom was put in a German concentration camp because she had helped Jewish people hide from the Nazis. Once the war was over Corrie developed a ministry and was invited all over the world to speak. She was already in her fifties, but she gave herself to her work for many years until she died.

One Sunday, when she was eighty, she spoke in a church in Denmark. After the service, two young women invited her to join them for lunch at their apartment. Corrie said, "Wonderful," and headed to their home.

She discovered there that they lived on the tenth floor and there was no elevator. She didn't think she could make it up the stairs as an eighty year old, but these women were so eager. Corrie decided to try.

By the fifth floor, she was gasping for breath, her heart was pounding, and her legs were giving out. She sank into a chair on one of the floors and was inwardly complaining bitterly to God. "Is this the day I go to heaven?"

But she felt God say, "Corrie, be patient with this. Something wonderful is waiting for you." So, she continued the hard climb with one young woman in front of her and one behind.

When she got to the apartment, the parents of one of the girls were there and neither one was a Christian. They were hungry to hear about Jesus and had been eagerly waiting for Corrie. She opened her Bible and began to explain how Jesus saves lives. Her words about the gospel were so touching to the parents that they both gave their lives to Christ right there.

Later in the day, when Corrie went down the stairs, she just prayed, "Thank you, Lord, for giving me the patience to go up these stairs. And next time, help me to listen to my own sermons about being willing, being patient enough, to go wherever you send me – even up ten flights of stairs."[23]

Corrie ten Boom brought two people into the family of God that day because she decided to be patient in several different ways. She had to be patient with her elderly body that was not so strong. She had to be patient with two young women getting her into the situation of needing to climb ten flights of stairs. She had to be patient with the climb, patient with people that needed teaching, and she had to be patient with a God who considers two people being saved at lunch to be more important than anything, even aches and pains.

I like this story because it presents the fact that we have a variety of things with which we need to be patient. People, physical pain, difficult situations, God – all these things are opportunities for us to be patient. But, what is patience exactly?

Being patient means that you can wait when there are delays without getting upset. You can bear with difficult people or situations without losing your temper or being angry. It means that you persevere. And it can also mean that you are understanding and tolerant.

Patience with People

Everyday someone gives us the opportunity to practice being patient with them, right? Whether it's a sloppy co-worker after whom you must clean up, or it's people using your things without asking, or someone being moody, whiny, bossy, or full of themselves, you are given a choice to be patient or not. Every day, there's someone who helps you practice taking a deep breath while praying, counting to ten, or going in the next room to blow off steam.

God's desire is for us to be patient with others. He does not want us to be inwardly bitter, or outwardly furious. He wants us to learn how to tolerate others without compromising our values. He wants us to keep going and not quit.

So, in other words, if you have a sloppy co-worker, it is fine to talk with them directly about the problem. Help them, if possible. Show them how to do the job better in a tactful way. What is not a good solution is blowing up and crushing them with your words or even going further than that. The way of a Christ follower is peace, working things out in peace.

One of the most famous verses in the Bible is 1 Corinthians 13:4 (NIV) where it says, "Love is patient. Love is kind." And when you put that verse together with something Jesus said (John 13:35 NIV), you know patience is a requirement for someone who claims to follow Him. He said, "By this everyone will know that you are my disciples, if you love one another."

If loving other people will convince them that we truly are Jesus' followers and if one of the aspects of love is that "it is patient," then we must be patient with people. And oh, it takes a lot of practice, doesn't it? And a lot of apologies along the way when we are impatient.

Let me tell you another story about a Christian leader and patience.

There was a great evangelist in the late 1800's named D.L. Moody. One night he was holding two services back to back. As the first crowd left he was near the front door to greet the second crowd coming in.

It was just at this point that a man approached Moody, "got in his face," and insulted him badly. Moody's temper flared, and he pushed the man down a short flight of steps.

The man was not hurt much, but Moody's friends wondered how on earth he could go on with the second service when people had witnessed his impatient behavior. They thought, "Mr. Moody has killed this service. Too many people saw what he did. No one will be influenced by a thing he has to say."

But Moody went forward. He stood up and said with a shaky voice, "Friends, before beginning this service tonight I want to confess that I just now gave in to my temper, outside the hall, and I was in the wrong. Just as I was coming in here this evening, I lost my temper with someone, and I want to confess my wrongdoing to all of you. If that man is still here who I pushed down in my anger, I want to ask for his forgiveness and I ask God to forgive me too. Now, let us pray."

Instead of having a bad meeting, people would say later that it was unusually moving and wonderful.[24]

We will meet many people who offend us like the man with Moody, or who are nuisances, annoying, or they have some other characteristic that gets on our "last nerve," but God will still say, "Have patience, learn patience."

And we must also have patience with God. There are times that we pray, and we ask for certain things, and the message we get from God is "not yet." Or we feel we just cannot hear Him. In those times, we must have patience and remember the Bible says He is for us and with us. We must patiently endure, waiting for God's timing.

Patience with Testing

Sometimes, the patience is needed with suffering. We have an illness, or a family member has an illness and healing hasn't come. Maybe, we are struggling with money problems, or are looking for a job. There are many times when you feel like, "I just can't take this situation another moment," and yet God would tell us, "Trust Me, worship, stay with Me. Things will resolve. Don't quit and keep a good attitude." We never know what God is doing "behind the scenes," but we must continue with that spark of unrelenting hope that says, "He is working."

Patience with Time Passing

And finally, sometimes we must just be patient with waiting, with time passing, with boredom. Perhaps, you're waiting in a line of traffic, a line in a store, or to be called for your turn at a clinic.

Sometimes we're just waiting for our turn and great patience is needed. Sometimes, we're waiting for something to happen and time just keeps going on and on.

Sometimes, the patience we need is just with having to watch time pass and in living with many ordinary, unexciting days. It's keeping steady day to day.

But, if we'll learn this skill, to wait gracefully, life will be so much more peaceful, and we'll avoid mistakes like flaring up with anger as Moody did, or rushing ahead of God and trying to make things happen when it's not the right time for them.

God's Patience with Us

As we struggle with this very hard skill – you know sometimes one of the people we most have to be patient with is ourselves – we need to remember God's great patience and love for us. Romans 5:8 says this: "But God showed His great love for us by sending Christ to die for us while we were still sinners." (NLT)

The greatest demonstration of patience ever was made was done by God. He didn't love us and enter our situation after we became perfect. We never could be perfect on our own. He came when we were difficult, rebellious people and gave us total forgiveness. He was totally patient with us and still is. He is God who is "gracious, and compassionate, slow to anger and rich in love." (Psalm 145:8 NIV) The "slow to anger" means God is patient. In fact, the Contemporary English Version of the Bible translates that phrase as "patient."

So be patient with yourself in this recovery process. Give yourself the time that's needed to get really strong in sobriety before moving on to the next season in your life. God has an amazing way of making up for what we think is a whole bunch of lost time. And, when you make the mistake of being impatient with others, apologize to God and apologize to them, then get back on your feet and keep trying. Be patient with you because *He* is patient with you.

Questions for the Small Group Session

1. What makes you impatient? Do you get impatient often?

2. How can you react differently and be patient instead? What tips do you have for the group about how to become more patient? How does Jesus help in this?

3. We've talked about fear in these studies. Do you think fear and impatience are connected?

4. Who has been really patient with you in the past and recently? What did that look like?

5. Sometimes people joke and say, "If you want to learn patience (or forgiveness), you must live in a community with roommates! Is living in a community helping you to become more patient or is it really challenging for you?

11

The Power of Forgiveness:
For God, Yourself, and Others

Key Verses

"I, even I, am he who blots out your transgressions, for my own sake, and remembers your sins no more." (Isaiah 43:25 NIV)

"Bear with each other and forgive one another if any of you has a grievance against someone. Forgive as the Lord forgave you." (Colossians 3:13 NIV)

Jacob said, "...to see your face is like seeing the face of God, now that you have received me favorably." (Genesis 33:10 NIV)

Key Issues for the Speaker to Consider

There is a scene in the movie, the Blind Side, the story of Michael Oher, the extremely poor kid from the projects who became a professional football player, where he reveals to the mother of the family who took him in, that he never had a bed growing up. She and her family have just created a bedroom for Michael in their home after taking him in as a homeless teenager.

Actress Sandra Bullock (portraying real life mother, Leigh Anne Tuohy) goes into the next room, shuts the door and cries.

When you minister in recovery settings, and if the primary background of the people you are working with is like Michael's, poor or very poor, addiction in the extended family, and so on, you will hear the same kind of stories and it breaks your heart.

The neglect, the lack, the abuse, the violence that many have endured creates these moments for you, in ministry, where you need to go into the next room, shut the door, and cry...and pray.

I confess that as I drive into the inner-city neighborhoods where I have ministered for several years now, there are days when I want to drive right back out. I don't feel strong enough to hear one more story of rape or abuse, abandonment, attempted murder, and so on that have happened in the lives of the people with whom I minister. Granted, not all personal histories are so dramatic, thank goodness, but there are enough of these horrible accounts of extreme behavior, that one's heart can get very heavy.

This is not to say that the same things don't happen in any community. Wicked behavior is no respecter of demographics. It happens everywhere. But when someone comes from a poor background, the escape routes out of trauma seem fewer.

And yet, with God, all things are possible.

It is very important to acknowledge the horror of these experiences people have gone through and yet, help them know that if they can grasp the biblical concept of forgiveness and practice it, they will be set free. You CAN walk out of your past. You can heal from old memories. Truly, we can forgive perpetrators who have done horrible things while not excusing or downplaying their horrible acts. We can forgive them even if we cannot continue to be close to them. And we can live in the power of the resurrection, not as victims.

I firmly believe that when we come to dwell on the magnificent beauty of God the Son, Jesus, begin to grasp much more fully all He accomplished on the cross for us, and how MUCH He loves us, we stop being "ticked off" by other people for petty things or being grievously, continually wounded about big stuff. Our awareness of His profound love and great plan for us makes us cut other people a lot of slack. We become able to forgive. Why? Because our present and future do not depend on them. They depend on Him.

> **Our awareness of His profound love and great plan for us makes us cut other people a lot of slack.**

And through Him, also, our own past is erased and forgotten. Isaiah 43:25, mentioned above, is only one of several verses that say, "God *chooses* to forget our sins." We have no need to stay mad at ourselves, at God, or at others. And we must NOT stay mad at ourselves, at God, or at others. To do so is to prolong our suffering and God does not intend for us to live a life of suffering because of unforgiveness.

You will have your work cut out for you, however, in convincing people who've seen some pretty awful stuff, that they should just let it go. We often do not forgive because we fear that that will let someone else "off the hook." Not only that, we fear they may celebrate their victory over us, or even worse, they may do the same thing yet again to us or someone else. It is important to teach that what the other person chooses to do is not the issue. What is important is what we choose to do.

There is an additional problem, in that, we may struggle with a desire for justice and to see the guilty get punished. To forgive someone is to release that need to see them punished, at least by us. This is not easy. We need God's help. Your recovery audience will truly need prayers for God's strength to move in them, so they can succeed in forgiving.

It is important to stress that God says several things about forgiveness in His Word.

1. We have been guilty and need forgiveness too. (Romans 3:23)

2. Jesus died a horrific death so that the *whole* world could be forgiven. (1 John 2:2)

3. Unless we forgive, God cannot forgive us. (Matthew 6:15)

4. God is the vindicator, the justice bringer. Not us. (Romans 12:19)

5. God has commanded us to bless our enemies. (Matthew 5:44)

6. Horrific things can be forgiven. We can get free of them. The story of Joseph, as you probably know, is a classic story in the Bible about forgiving the unforgiveable. Joseph's own brothers sold him into slavery. They lied to their father and said Joseph was dead. The wife of Joseph's owner in Egypt lied about him and accused him of rape. He was thrown into prison. A man he reached out to for help, who he helped in prison, the king's cupbearer, forgot all about him for two years, once released. So, Joseph languished in prison two extra years. (Genesis 37, 39 and 40)

7. But Joseph kept a right heart and attitude and was trustworthy even as a slave and a prisoner. *God* vindicated him and lifted him out of prison to a place of prominence and a place where he could thrive and do good work. God will restore our lives, too, after we are hurt if we will fully trust Him and practice forgiveness. (Genesis 50:19-21).

How do you know when you have totally forgiven someone else?

You will stop thinking about the person and their wrongs. You will no longer have repeating conversations with them in your head filled with "what you should have said." You will *not* tell others about their wrongs. You will stop thinking of ways to punish them and you will not attempt to punish them. You will be able to say with all sincerity, "I forgive them." You will feel God's peace and presence with you. All bitterness will be gone. Recovery goes so much more smoothly without grudges.[25]

Prayer for the Speaker and the Talk

Oh Lord, You know how hard it is for us to get over the pain we sometimes feel from others' ways of treating us. We wrestle, and we struggle to let go of the hurt and then replace it with forgiveness. We also hurt others and find it difficult at times to say the words of humility, "I'm sorry." Precious Spirit, I pray for this speaker right now, if struggling with hurt, to feel it lift by Your power at work in him or her. Let forgiveness and the joy of remaining close to You through obedience be their primary impulse. Help this speaker to remember that they are forgiven and loved by You and that this forgiveness took place already, more than two thousand years ago. Help them to receive the reality of it even more fully into their heart and the knowledge that they are precious and honored in Your sight. By fully accessing Your love and forgiveness for themselves, help them to radiate that before their audience. Help them to lead those whom You have given them to teach to a full willingness to be practitioners of forgiveness in Your strength. In Jesus' name, Amen

Sample Talk:

Introduction

Years ago, I remember being invited to be a guest speaker in a women's Bible study at another church. A lot of women attended this short-term study. I was also asked to lead one of their small groups. Only a few weeks into this event, I was told by one of the leaders that a woman in my group had said, "If she had to be in my group one moment longer, she wasn't coming anymore."

I was stunned. I had only just met this woman.

From my perspective, I thought the group was going so well, that we were having excellent discussions. I thought about my leadership of the group, considered if I had been offensive or arrogant or in any way, had not acted properly. I could not think of anything I had done or said, particularly where this woman was concerned. I felt I had been warm and kind.

It was hurtful and embarrassing to me to be spoken of this way. And it threatened future collaborations, I thought. But, we made it possible for the woman to switch groups. I only hoped she was not telling others in the gathering her thoughts about me, poisoning the waters even more.

I will tell you truthfully, I was tempted to dwell on it and feel offense towards her. I was tempted to avoid her. And then I prayed. "Lord, I hurt over this. Help me." I wish she was the only one, but things like this happen in churches. People come in to churches carrying wounds and seeing offenses in other people because of their filters caused by previous wounds. Somehow, I had stepped on this woman's toes for reasons I could not understand. And now, she had hurt me, and since I am a leader, she was not the first to cause me hurt in my years of leading.

I began to pray with great intensity. "Lord, don't let me have any offense where she is concerned. Help me to release her, forgive her totally, and say nothing more to anyone about what has happened." I prayed this way for a few weeks. The good news is that through these prayers, God helped me. It was not long before I felt nothing more regarding her rejection. And when I saw her, I was able to warmly say hello with sincerity. I totally let go of my pain and totally forgave her. I said nothing more to anyone about it.

Perhaps I *had* said something to her or responded to her in a way that had rubbed her wrong. I may have been insensitive and not realized it. Perhaps she was going through some really difficult situations. Maybe I reminded her of someone. I will never know. But, the important thing is, the Lord helped me. He set me free from unforgiveness. He made me free of pain. But, I was faithful and obedient to come to Him in prayer and to follow His teachings, as best I could, about forgiveness.

How many times do we have these kinds of episodes in our lives?

We All Get Hurt

We have them a lot because there are a lot of people in our lives, from family, to co-workers, to neighbors, to people on the street – there are so many opportunities for people to hurt us in small ways all the way to huge, seemingly unforgiveable ways. If we lived as hermits, we might not have to worry about forgiveness, except for forgiving ourselves. But, we don't live as hermits, most of us, so there are lots of opportunities to be wounded by others. And for us to wound others. We get plenty of opportunity to practice forgiveness.

I want to tell you a Bible story about two brothers tonight, Jacob and Esau. You may know it well or it may be brand new to you. But it is a great story about what can happen, even between brothers, that needs forgiving.

There was a moment in their lives when Esau wanted to kill Jacob. It was so bad that Jacob even fled their country to get away from Esau. This is how it happened:

Unforgiveness Causes Problems

Jacob and Esau were two brothers who had problems even before birth! The Bible says that the babies wrestled with each other even inside their mother Rebekah. (Genesis 25:22) When the boys were born, Esau came out first, but Jacob was holding onto his heel, trying to get ahead of him, I guess. (Gen. 25:26) Esau became a hunter, an outdoorsman, while Jacob was happy to stay at home among the tents. (Genesis 25:27) Isaac, their father, made Esau his favorite, but Rebekah, their mom, liked Jacob best. (Genesis 25:28) Not good, right?

The two major episodes of an ongoing battle between the brothers are the stories of Jacob taking Esau's birthright and his blessing.

One day Esau came in from outside and he was so hungry. He asked for some of Jacob's stew. Jacob, ever the clever manipulator at this point of his life, said, "Sell me your birthright and I'll give you the stew." Esau, who had been born first of these twins, said, "Fine, you can have my birthright, now give me my food," and he got bread and lentil stew. Being firstborn came with many rights and privileges in ancient Israel, and Jacob manipulated Esau right out of them. But, notice Esau was willing to give up these blessings for a mere dinner!

The more aggravating wrong happened when daddy Isaac was much older and going blind. He wanted his son Esau to come see him with some game he would hunt and cook. Then Isaac planned to give him his blessing after a great dinner.

Rebekah, however, overheard the request. Loving Jacob best, she told him to put on some of his brother's clothes and to disguise his arms with animal skins as Esau was a hairy man. She then cooked a goat and gave it to Jacob to bring into Isaac. Isaac was somewhat questioning about who he had before his weak eyes but smelling the clothing and feeling the "hairy arms," he accepted that it must be Esau and he gave his fatherly blessing to Jacob. (Genesis 27)

In the blessing, Isaac made Jacob ruler over his brothers and other family. Esau was bitter and upset, once he got back and figured out what had happened. He begged his father to also bless him, but what his father told him about his future, as a result of this lost first born blessing, was dismal.

Esau was furious and said, "The days of mourning for my father are near; then I will kill my brother Jacob." (Genesis 27:41 NIV)

Rebekah once again stepped in on Jacob's behalf and thwarted Esau's plan. She sent Jacob to her brother's home in Haran. Jacob fled from a brother bent on killing him. He moved in with his uncle Laban.

A lot of years passed. Jacob served his uncle Laban, married his two daughters, and had many children. He had conflict with this part of the family too, but eventually, Jacob heard God speak to him saying, "Go back to the land of your fathers and to your relatives, and I will be with you." (Genesis 31:3 NIV)

God is in Forgiveness

As Jacob approached the region where he would find Esau, he sent ahead servants with many flocks, hoping to get on Esau's good side. He prayed and reminded God of His promises that, he, Jacob, would be a success and asked God for protection. As he got near to Esau who had four hundred men with him, Jacob lined up his wives and children behind him, and with a lot of fear, he went on to meet Esau.

Then, the most surprising thing happened. Esau ran up to meet him, threw his arms around him, kissed him, and cried with joy. (Genesis 33:4)

Esau wondered why Jacob had sent so many herds to him. Jacob said he had hoped to please him. Esau said that he already had plenty of his own herds and that Jacob should keep them himself. Then one of the most beautiful lines in the Bible is spoken. Jacob said that seeing the forgiveness and acceptance coming from Esau was like "seeing the face of God." (Genesis 33:10 NIV) Imagine that – the brother who had wanted to kill him, now seemed like God to Jacob, because he was full of forgiveness.

How true that is – when one person forgives another, especially if what has happened between them has been a *very* difficult thing, it is a moment when the presence of God is very real. Why? Because God is love. And God's whole attitude towards the human race has been to forgive us and restore us to relationship with Him through the cross of Jesus Christ. God is love. He is forgiveness.

We Must Forgive

God asks us to be the kind of people who are ready to say, "I forgive you," all the time. Why? Because He did it for us. That doesn't mean we excuse every kind of behavior or fail to notice someone's lack of repentance. We need wisdom in the way we handle these situations. If someone does not repent, you can still seek to let go of your bitterness.

We were forgiven roughly two thousand years ago. Jesus bore our burden, so we wouldn't have to pay, to face the wrath of God against sin. He let us off the hook. We need to turn and let those who have harmed us be free if they are sorry and be free even if they are not.

One last Bible story makes this point. This story is called the parable of the Unmerciful Servant. It is found in Matthew 18:23-35. Jesus was prompted to tell this story when Peter asked him how many times he had to forgive a brother or sister who sinned against him. "Seven times?" Peter suggested. Jesus replied, I tell you, not seven times, but seventy-seven times." (Matthew 18:23-35 NIrV)

Then Jesus told a story. He said:

The kingdom of heaven is like a king who wanted to collect all the money owed him. As the king began to do it, a man who owed him 10,000 bags of gold was brought to him. The man was not able to pay. So, his master gave an order. The man, his wife, his children, and all he owned had to be sold to pay back what he owed.

Then the servant fell on his knees in front of him. "Give me time," he begged. "I'll pay everything back." His master felt sorry for him. He forgave him what he owed and let him go.

But then that servant went out and found one of the other servants who owed him 100 silver coins. He grabbed him and began to choke him. "Pay back what you owe me!" he said.

The other servant fell on his knees. "Give me time," he begged him. "I'll pay it back."

But the first servant refused. Instead he went and had the man thrown into prison. The man would be held there until he could pay back what he owed. The other servants saw what had happened and were very angry. They went and told their master everything that had happened.

Then the master called the first servant in. "You evil servant," he said. "I forgave all that you owed me because you begged me to. Shouldn't you have had mercy on the other servant just as I had mercy on you?" In anger his master handed him over to the jailers. He would be punished until he paid back everything he owed.

This is how my Father in heaven will treat each of you unless you forgive your brother or sister from your heart.

This is a hard story because it is saying, "You must forgive because, in Christ, you have been forgiven far more. If you have come to believe in Jesus, He saved you from eternal death and moved you to eternal life."

You may think there are some things just too hard to forgive, I know, but I can think of countless stories of people forgiving all kinds of terrible things. I know a father who forgave his son's murderer and now ministers to inmates in prison. I know a man who was innocent but imprisoned for twenty-five years. He has forgiven everyone for this wrong and is now a pastor. I read the story of a man made blind by a teenager throwing large rocks off a freeway overpass. He forgave him while visiting him in prison.[26] There is a story of Corrie ten Boom, the Christian leader held in Nazi concentration camps, mentioned in a previous chapter, who found the courage to shake hands and forgive the guard who had been so cruel to her, her sister, and others.[27]

So many stories can be told of people who have forgiven the unforgiveable and found great freedom in doing it. Sometimes, someone doesn't say I am sorry or make any amends. You can still release them in your heart and leave them to God, walking away from your own captivity and bitterness. It is *so* worth it. You will love how you feel when you are free from unforgiveness and most importantly, you'll be in sync with your Father in heaven.

209

Questions for the Small Group Session

1. How easy is it for you to forgive someone when they hurt you? Are you trying to forgive someone right now?

2. Do you find yourself easily offended or irritated over small things? What steps can you take to stop that?

3. Do you fear that if you forgive someone totally, they will "get away with 'it'?" Do you feel like you have got to stay angry to make sure they feel very sorry or so that they get the punishment they deserve?

4. Does praying for people who've hurt you help you to have more peace? Are you able to pray for "enemies?"

5. What is the message of the Parable of the Unmerciful Servant?

Pray with group members who may express real pain from things that have been done to them from which they have not yet recovered.

12

Don't Quit Five Minutes Before Your Miracle

Key Verses

Hannah said, "'May your servant find favor in your eyes.' Then she went her way and ate something, and her face was no longer downcast." (1 Sam. 1:18 NIV)

"Rejoice always, pray continually, give thanks in all circumstances; for this is God's will for you in Christ Jesus." (1 Thessalonians 5:16-17 NIV)

"...the cheerful heart has a continual feast." (Proverbs 15:15b NIV)

Issues for the Speaker to Consider

(Note: This could be the night to especially have some people share their testimonies of success in recovery, either live or via video. These stories will cause faith to rise in the room.)

It is much easier to look forward to one's earthly future confidently if one has a good job, a home, a car, and a well-stocked 401 K than if one has no money, no bank account, no job, no home, numerous relational bridges burned behind them, etc.

I am speaking in a natural way, of course. But this is the struggle in our lives to figure out from where our security and identity are going to come. We can learn, in our walk with God, to take each day a step at a time and come to believe fiercely that God will provide, no matter where we are in life. We can come to believe that He will make a way where there is no way. Furthermore, we can gain the correct eternal perspective, that it isn't for this brief life alone that we were made. God has placed "eternity in the human heart." (Ecclesiastes 3:11 NIV) "Our citizenship is in heaven. And we eagerly await a Savior from there, the Lord Jesus Christ." (Philippians 3:20 NIV)

Nevertheless, speaking realistically, it can be very hard for someone who's lost most everything through addiction, and who didn't have much to begin with, hear you say, "Trust in God. Have hope in Him. Your future can be bright here and you will dwell with Him eternally too." It can sound way too foolish and simplistic. Especially if they are getting into their thirties, forties, fifties and on. They may feel the future closing in and that hope-filled talk may feel like it doesn't match up with their day to day struggles. Many listening can believe that God is a big part of the problem. They may believe that He has been causing their bad luck and their losses. He's the reason that they showed up to a recovery community with their belongings in a trash bag. And, there will be those who may be subject to depression, panic and anxiety attacks or other troubled states of mind. Having hope may seem like a totally unrealistic response.

But whether someone has a healthy retirement account, or no bank account, a million bucks or no bucks, the call of the Bible is for all of us to turn to God in absolute trust and dependence for our earthly and spiritual needs. The reason the Twenty-Third Psalm of the Bible has been a classic, loved by believers and known by non-believers, is that it evokes this lifestyle of resting, believing in, and feeling utterly protected by a good God leading us to a good future.

In the Twenty-Third Psalm, God is portrayed like a shepherd from the Middle East who will go to any length to protect his sheep, treating them like a father. Good shepherds in this region are actually like this, therefore, the words are very accurate.[28] "The Lord is my Shepherd. I shall not want. He makes me lie down in green pastures. He leads me beside still waters. He restores my soul..." (Psalm 23:1-3a NKJV)

The Lord is also portrayed as a Mediterranean host in this Psalm, the one who sets a table before us in the presence of our enemies. He "anoints our heads with oil and gives us overflowing cups. Goodness and mercy are going to follow us all the days of our lives," thanks to the care of our heavenly host, God. (Paraphrase of Psalm 23:5b-6a)

When you lead people to trusting in the God of the Bible, revealed through Jesus Christ, by the work of the Holy Spirit, they will begin to look at their situations with spiritual eyes and look beyond the struggles of the current day, believing a powerful and able God knows and will get them through it. They get the ability to look at trouble as temporary. Not only that, but in the struggle, they trust that God will carry them.

"No one who hopes in you will ever be put to shame." (Psalm 25:3a NIV)

How do you, with God's help, get them to that place of trust? How can you get them past being dejected, angry, or cynical, thinking things will never change, feeling that tomorrow is just more of yesterday's leftovers? How can you get them to the powerful faith that will make them hope relentlessly like Abraham (Romans 4:18-25), even as things worsen? What do you tell them to keep them from quitting just before their breakthrough?

There is a beautiful verse that says:

> **"Return to your fortress, you prisoners of hope; even now I announce that I will restore twice as much to you." (Zechariah 9:12 NIV)**

What a blessed idea that is, being so hopeful that you are a *prisoner* of hope and knowing you love and serve a God, if you are a believer, who restores double to His beleaguered ones.

Teaching the Word of God diligently is part of helping them to become faith-filled, always hopeful people. There are so many promises of God in the Bible. When people begin to grab a hold of these words and decree (speak) them over themselves and pray them, their lives change. I often say to people, "You must be like a cow chewing its cud on this Word of God. Chew on it over and over again so that it truly gets 'digested' – you totally take in the words and their meaning! The words must become established in you so that their power changes you."

"For the word of God is living and powerful, and sharper than any two-edged sword," just as Hebrews 4:12 (NKJV) states. It has supernatural power to transform us and our circumstances. Therefore, to be a "prisoner of hope," the Bible must be front and center in our lives.

You cannot live in rebellion towards God and hope that the promises of God from the Bible will work for you. To have the benefits of hoping in God, one must be compliant with His Word. We have to hear the words about obedience, purity, and making amends with others and *practice* them as well as listen for and procure His grace and help. We have a part to play in what happens in our future. You must teach this too. Even the hard sayings of the Bible. The "whole counsel of God" must be taught and followed, as it says in Acts 20:27.

Sharing testimonies of people who have been in dire straits, but who were rescued by God is tremendously helpful in building up hope and faith. "If it happened to them, it can happen to me!" becomes the listeners' response. Having these people share their testimonies themselves, in person if possible, is even more powerful than via videos. This needs to be a very regular part of your gatherings – hearing what belief in Jesus Christ has done in the lives of broken people. And teach your community members to celebrate other peoples' success. It is part of setting themselves up for breakthrough too. Envy doesn't aid breakthrough!

You need to help them understand what Jesus meant when He said, "Truly I tell you, unless you change and become like little children, you will never enter the kingdom of heaven." (Matthew 18:3 NIV)

What are little children like? They are ready to be cared for and directed by those who are bigger and stronger. They are playful, ready to give and receive love. They are simple, mostly non-judgmental. You enter the kingdom of heaven by laying down your way of doing business and thinking, instead letting God love and direct you. Being childlike involves surrender. But, as Jesus said, if we can be simple and childlike, we begin to experience the amazing wonders of God. The kingdom of heaven is a place of miracles.

You can help your recovery community or class become more hopeful by modeling it for them and stressing gratitude. It is fortunate that gratitude is often the topic in recovery communities and it has always been a component of Twelve Step recovery groups. In the 1 Thessalonian 5 verses above, the instruction is given to be thankful in all circumstances. How does that mesh together with hope?

When you are saying thanks daily for even the smallest of good things, you remind yourself that you have been helped already. You are making progress. Things are moving forward. You are not forgotten. These ideas feed hope and help the person in recovery believe that they will continue to move ahead, and they will make their goals.

This thankfulness ties into one more hope builder and that is remembrance. It is so important to remember what God has already brought you through. Not everyone likes to write things down, but if you can

> **It is so important to remember what God has already brought you through.**

encourage those you are teaching to try and do this, it will help them. On a difficult day, they can go back and see something wonderful that happened and give God the thanks for it. Our spirits lift when we recall previous help and God-touched experiences.

I remember when I entered seminary, we had to write down something that God did for us in our past. The point was made by our instructor that many times we don't recognize God's hand in our experiences until we make it through them and time has passed. Hopefully, as people mature in faith, they get so they do recognize moment to moment God's presence and constant help, but until that time, recalling past help gives a person hope for the future.

Prayer for the Speaker and the Talk

Lord, your Word says, "Hope deferred makes the heart sick, but a longing fulfilled is a tree of life." (Proverbs 13:12 NIV) Help this speaker to have such hope in their own heart about their own longings. Bring fulfillment of promises into their own life in every area. Help them to blow on the spark of hope in the group to whom they are ministering by giving a truly uplifting talk. Give them the words to build faith and nourish dreams. Help them to encourage their people and to see each one as special and beloved to You. Father, may every member of this recovery community walk out after this talk with joy and a lightness in their hearts, ready to tackle a new day and to keep going even when the going is tough. Don't let them run from the work of getting well. We thank You, Lord, and ask for Your powerful anointing on this speaker. In Jesus' name. Amen

Sample Talk:

Introduction

Have you ever felt just broken down and hopeless, like nothing's ever going to change? Of course, you have. We all have. I want to share a story with you tonight about a woman who was just miserable and felt hopeless, all because she wanted to have a child.

You may know this Bible story about a woman named Hannah. Hannah was married to a man named Elkanah. And as was done in those times, Elkanah had another wife named Peninnah.

Peninnah had children, but Hannah had not been able to have children and she was sad.

Every year they went up to a place called Shiloh for a special time of worship. Elkanah would sacrifice animals as was the custom in those days and he would give some of the meat to Peninnah and her sons and daughters, but he would give a double portion to Hannah. He loved her and he also was sympathetic about her childlessness.

Peninnah would make fun of Hannah and irritate her until the point that Hannah would cry. Then Elkanah would talk to her in his clumsy way. He would say, "Why are you weeping? Aren't I worth ten sons?"

This went on for a long time. Hannah felt hopeless, sad. Many people long to have children, but in her day, it was so important. People would think that God had pushed you away if you didn't have children. The two great blessings they had in her day were children and land.

Make Up Your Mind to Do Something

Hannah finally had enough of feeling blue and miserable, of thinking nothing would ever change. She had to *get her hope back*!

The bible says she STOOD UP! And the Hebrew word for this means she literally jumped out of her seat and firmly planted both feet on the ground. You might think of Wonder Woman striking a pose. Hannah did not get out of her seat meekly and mildly. She stood up so suddenly and firmly that maybe some things got knocked over. Maybe she broke a vase! She got out of that seat ready to do business.

Sometimes when we feel hopeless, we have got to make a decision, "I can keep thinking like this or I can get up and plant my feet on the ground and start to take action in my heart and perhaps in my life to rekindle hope.

Make Up Your Mind to Pray

What Hannah did was she marched over to the sanctuary and went in, brushing hurriedly past the priest, Eli, who was sitting at the doorway. She was still weeping, but she was steely and determined to see something happen. She knelt to pray and began to pour out her heart to God. She said, "LORD Almighty, if you will only look on your servant's misery and remember me, and not forget your servant but give her a son, then I will give him to the LORD for all the days of his life..." (1 Samuel 1:11 NIV)

She kept praying fervently to God. The words were in her heart and her lips were moving, but she was not making a sound. Eli made a wrong assumption. He thought she had been drinking and accused her of it. (You have to wonder why he, a priest, couldn't recognize strong, passionate prayer!)

Hannah told him that she was not drunk, not a wicked woman, but she was there to do something about her anguish and grief. She was there to do something about feeling stuck and hopeless.

You and I have the greatest tool in the world for chasing away hopeless feelings and that is prayer. How long do you have to pray to see what you want happen? Do you have to cry and pray in the same manner as Hannah?

My answer would be pray until you feel satisfied in the Lord. Pray until you feel like you have really shared your heart. Pray until you feel His presence. Perhaps worshipping Him with your favorite songs will soothe your heart. Do what you need to do to put the matter in God's hands, and to feel hope rise again. The main thing is believing Him that He is good, He cares, and He is listening. It isn't so much about getting the answer as it is getting restored and stabilized in peace.

Leave It in God's Hands

Then leave it with Him. Don't take your troubles back. The Bible says, "Cast all your anxiety upon him because he cares for you." (1 Peter 5:7 NIV) Leave the matter with Him and believe He will get to work and even release His angels to do their part in the matter. *But, don't quit five minutes before your miracle.* It's when things seem hardest, perhaps when you are saying, "But I've been trying for *so* long," that your breakthrough is right around the corner. It may truly be just five minutes away. Hang on to hope and watch for what God will do. No matter what, He's going to walk with you and walk this matter out. Above all else, don't let go of hope and don't let go of Him!

And by the way, the next year, Hannah had her amazing baby boy, Samuel, her first child, who became a great prophet in Israel. Since she had promised him to God, God then gave her five more children. What a promise-keeping God our God is!!

Questions for the Small Group Session

1. When you look back on your life, when was there a time where you thought there was no way out of some trouble, but you made it? Do you see God's hand in that now?

2. When you have difficulties today, are you able to turn to God and say, "Help me, Lord, without You, I can't make it?"

3. When someone here in the community is really struggling, feeling hopeless, how do you encourage them?

4. What do you think about the story of Hannah and how *she* got over being sad and feeling hopeless?

5. There's a quote often credited to President Lincoln that says, "Most people are about as happy as they decide to be." It is not known for sure whether Lincoln said it or not, but do you think you can make up your mind to be happy and hopeful? How can you do that?

A Final Word to Pastors and Leaders

If you are a pastor, you may be thinking about how to offer recovery ministry in your church. You may have thought, "I just need to invite an Alcoholics Anonymous group to meet in one of our classrooms or find some leaders and launch a Celebrate Recovery program one night during the week."

I would like to suggest, instead of thinking of recovery as just another "add on program," that you first consider the "climate" of your church. Does your community believe in the present-day healing ministry of Jesus Christ? Do you believe He can heal anything? Is there openness to relationship with the Holy Spirit who makes us aware of Jesus and His ministry? Are you able to preach and teach about the Holy Spirit? Are there expectations of the gifts of the Spirit being demonstrated in your church?

If this sort of a climate is present, it will be much easier to begin to speak about the need to open your hearts and your doors to people in recovery as we are all in some sort of "recovery." If this New Testament climate is not present, if instead, it feels as if there is an environment of surface propriety and moralism instead, it is time to preach grace, remind people of the universal need for the cross, and begin to lay the groundwork of an expectation for healing ministry.

When the people have been sufficiently prepared, you can begin to lead them as a group to reaching out to everyone, to ministering more frequently and effectively beyond your walls and to becoming a welcoming, integrating community for those in recovery. You can then begin to think about logistics for further implementing this ministry as your community's way of life.

If you minister in a jail, prison, or recovery facility, consider truly offering Jesus as the way out of addiction, presenting Christian faith-based materials without apology.

I come out of a Wesleyan background, so small groups where love and accountability can grow are huge to me as a way of spiritual formation for people. I believe in stable small groups where people begin to really get to know one another and do life together within a church or recovery facility. Utilizing the lessons of this book and other materials, people can grow through their discussions and prayers with each other. You can dedicate a teaching/small group time or times to this approach – recovery through Jesus Christ - as you draw people with this need into the life of your church or work with people in a recovery facility.

But what is paramount in this age is to preach Jesus to all people. He is *the* Answer. In this time of a devastating plague of drug use, Jesus is *the* Liberator who frees. He Himself said,

> The Spirit of the Lord is on me, because he has anointed me to proclaim good news to the poor. He has sent me to proclaim freedom for the prisoners and recovery of sight for the blind, to set the oppressed *free*, to proclaim the year of the Lord's favor.

These are the words found in Luke 4:18-19 (NIV) which Jesus spoke from the scroll of Isaiah to announce the beginning of His ministry and what would characterize it. These words of anointing are also meant for us who follow Him as we consider the pressing need in this modern time to wipe out drug addiction. This is no time to be timid or lukewarm. We cannot temper our words so that they keep us safe from unpopularity. If ever there was a time to be bold again with the Gospel of Jesus Christ, it is now. If ever we needed to be crystal clear about who the Holy Spirit is and about the power that comes from on high and can dwell in us, it is now. People are dying in a variety of ways from drugs all over the world. Whether it is in a shootout among drug cartels in Mexico, a border agent being gunned down in the USA, or an addict overdosing in a motel room, people are dying. Families are being split apart. People are being financially ruined by the cost of addiction or the burden of treatment costs.

There are many approaches to helping people get free of drugs and many care about this issue. Seeing programs and initiatives launched from varying governmental levels is heartening, but what is needed in this age is a return to trust in the power that comes from God and the radical transformation of life that comes through the cross. This, I would argue, has not been trusted enough. We have thought that other means would be more effective for this problem. Yet, we see a landscape still littered with relapse and hopelessness.

So, I will just close with these second verse lyrics from the 1969 hymn tune, *There's a Spirit in the Air*, by hymn writer Brian A. Wren:

Lose your shyness, find your tongue;

Tell the world what God has done:

God in Christ has come to stay,

We can see his power today.

"Lose your shyness, find your tongue." Speak up and teach, demonstrate, and impart the redemptive ministry of Jesus Christ through the power of the Holy Spirit in the love of the Father. Help people to be permanently and truly free.

ABOUT THE AUTHOR

Dr. Pam Morrison became an ordained minister and prepared for a conventional path of serving in pastoral leadership in churches. She trained at St. Paul School of Theology in Kansas City, and Gordon-Conwell Theological Seminary in Charlotte, North Carolina. As a pastor formed out of the Methodist tradition, where pastors are moved more frequently, she served six churches either as an associate pastor or a lead pastor. As the Holy Spirit began to move in her life more and more, this pathway was drastically altered.

Pam began to minister to incarcerated people in 2008 as a Prison Fellowship volunteer. She found her heart greatly moved by the women with whom she engaged who were serving sentences in the Leavenworth, Kansas area. Most, if not all of them, were imprisoned because of drug related offenses. As Pam listened to their stories, the heartbreak of their childhoods, their longings for their own children, often no longer in their custody, her desire to minister Jesus Christ to men and women trying to escape addiction and an endless cycle of jail or prison time grew. The fire of that desire was further fanned by recovering addicts coming to the church she was leading, at that time, in increasing numbers.

In 2011, she left local church pastoral leadership for good and began to minister with addicted people and those coming out of jail and prison wherever God led her to find them. She has primarily served at the Healing House recovery community (www.healinghousekc.org) as a volunteer pastor for the last seven years and has also been part of the healing prayer team from Heartland Healing Rooms in the Kansas City area (www.heartlandhealingrooms.org). The Heartland Healing Rooms, founded by Lee and Doris Harms, are part of the International Association of Healing Rooms, led by Cal and Michelle Pierce, out of Spokane, Washington, a ministry founded in the tradition of John G. Lake's healing rooms. The Heartland Healing rooms minister at Hope City (www.hopecitykc.org), as one of their locations, another recovery community, associated with the International House of Prayer. It is this emphasis on the healing ministry of Christ, both inner healing and physical healing that Pam brings to her ministry. She shares healing prayer, pastoral counseling, teaching and preaching with those who are in recovery.

Additionally, Pam ministers overseas with preaching and healing prayer. She is currently partnering with Cuban pastors and missionaries to aid them in their ministries. Her ministry has taken her to Peru, Nicaragua, and Brazil multiple times also. She welcomes the opportunity to preach the gospel in power and to pray for healing wherever God leads.

Pam and her husband, David, live in the Overland Park, Kansas area. She has two children (four, counting their wonderful spouses) and five beautiful grandchildren.

To contact Dr. Morrison or to schedule her as a speaker:
email: revpmorrison21@gmail.com
www.pammorrisonministries.com

[1] NIH. (2017, April 24). *Trends & Statistics*. Retrieved June 17, 2018, from National Institute of Drug Abuse: https://www.drugabuse.gov/related-topics/trends-statistics

[2] Chadwick, S. (2000). *The Way to Pentecost.* Fort Washington, PA: CLC Publications.

[3] Prince, J. (2008). Destined to Reign. Tulsa, OK: Harrison House.

[4] This is the story of Danny Velasco which has been told many times at the Brooklyn Tabernacle Church in New York City. A video of his testimony is included on their DVD album entitled "I'm Amazed That You Love Me."

[5] This story is from Talk 6 of the Alpha course entitled, "Who is the Holy Spirit?"

[6] Chadwick, S. (2000). *The Way to Pentecost.* Fort Washington, PA: CLC Publications.

[7] Kandiah, K. (2015, March 5). The Church is growing, and here are the figures that prove it. Retrieved June 20, 2018, from Christian Today: https://www.christiantoday.com/article/a-growing-church-why-we-should-focus-on-the-bigger-picture/49362.htm

[8] Note on Galatians 2:21, New Spirit-Filled Life Bible, New King James Version, 2002, 1633.

[9] The song, "They will know we are Christians" was released in 2005 by Jars of Clay.

[10] Wurmbrand, R. (1998). Tortured for Christ. Bartlesville, OK: Living Sacrifice Book Company.

[11] Murray, A. (1984). The Spirit of Christ. New Kensington, PA: Whitaker House.

[12] These descriptions of thinking errors based on Dr. Stanton Samenow's work are described in a small pamphlet called "Corrective Thinking Process," 2007. The pamphlet is distributed through the website http://www.truthought.com.

[13] Souza, K. (2017). Soul Decrees. Maricopa, AZ: Eleven Eleven Enterprises.

[14] Souza, K. (2017). Soul Decrees. Maricopa, AZ: Eleven Eleven Enterprises.

[15] Sermons.com . (n.d.). Optimism. Retrieved June 12, 2018, from Sermon Illustration: http://www.sermonillustrations.com/a-z/o/optimism.htm

[16] Twain, M. (1922). Puddn'head Wilson. New York: P.F. Collier & Sons Company.

[17] Easton M.A., D.D., M. G. (1897). Temptation. Illustrated Bible Dictionary, Third Edition. Thomas Nelson. Retrieved from https://www.biblestudytools.com/dictionaries/eastons-bible-dictionary/temptation.html

[18] Disciple. (n.d.). Retrieved from Merriam-Webster: https://www.merriam-webster.com/dictionary/disciple

[19] Wimber, J. (1987). Power Healing. New York: Harper Collins.

[20] Baumchen, H. (2017, March 28). Overcoming Resentment and Bitterness. Retrieved June 21, 2018, from Journey to Recovery: https://blog.journeytorecovery.com/overcoming-resentment-and-bitterness/

[21] darash. (n.d.). Retrieved from Blue Letter Bible: https://www.blueletterbible.org/lang/lexicon/lexicon.cfm?Strongs=H1875&t=KJV

[22] Speigel, J. S. (2010, February 23). The Virtue of Patience: Waiting without complaining. Christian Bible Studies. Retrieved May 21, 2018, from https://www.christianitytoday.com/biblestudies/articles/spiritualformation/virtue-of-patience.html

[23] A Living Sacrifice. (2000). In R. J. Morgan, Nelson's Complete Book of Stories, Illustrations, and Quotes (p. 39). Nashville: Thomas Nelson Publishers.

[24] How D.L. Moody Dealt with Anger. (2000). In R. J. Morgan, Nelson's Complete Book of Stories, Illustrations, and Quotes (p. 30). Nashville: Thomas Nelson Publishers.

[25] Kendall, R. T. (2007). Total Forgiveness. Lake Mary, Fl: Charisma House.

[26] Wang, R. (2014, August 3). Columbus man forgave rock thrower who blinded him. CantonRep.com. Retrieved from http://www.cantonrep.com/article/20140803/NEWS/140809799

[27] The Unfrozen Hand. (2000). In R. J. Morgan, Nelson's Complete Book of Stories, Illustrations, and Quotes (p. 315). Nashville: Thomas Nelson Publishers.

[28] Laniak, T. S. (2007). While Shepherds Watch Their Flock: Forty Daily Reflections on Biblical Leadership. Shepherd Leader Publications.

When I feel like GOD is disappointed in me...
When the voice in my mind tells me I am a
  failure and will never be fruitful...
Focus on GOD's faithfulness not my faithlessness.
Jesus loves me. The Father loves me. The Holy
spirit reminds me that GOD will never give
up on me or abandon me. I am His
workmanship... He will complete the work
He has begun in me. Jesus is the Author
and finisher of my Faith.